BARLEY IS BETTER

Rosemary K. Newman
C. Walter Newman

Barley is Better

Rosemary K. Newman and C. Walter Newman

Hardcover ISBN 978-1-77342-004-2
Paperback ISBN 978-1-77342-018-9

Produced by IndieBookLauncher.com
www.IndieBookLauncher.com
Cover Design and Interior Layout by Saul Bottcher

Photos
Recipe photos by Rebecca Soulé.
Barley field photos by Erik Petersen / Bozeman Daily Chronicle.

BARLEY
is
BETTER

· ROSEMARY *and* WALTER NEWMAN ·

This book is dedicated to the farmer-growers who produce barley and the millers who process it into food ingredients.

❦ CONTENTS ❦

About This Book

Recipes

References

WHY THIS BOOK?

Our aim in writing this book is to share with other folks the really good things about barley, an almost-forgotten food.

When we mention barley as a food, "I like barley in soup" is the usual response. Most people are not aware of barley's versatility, nor do they realize the exceptional nutritional and health benefits of eating barley.

This book contains over 150 delicious recipes, including detailed nutrition information, that will allow you to include this fabulous grain in your every-day meals. More than 100 of the recipes are also available in vegan form, developed and individually tested by a vegan nutritionist.

The following few pages explain how to handle and prepare barley. Throughout the book, you'll also find facts about the origin, composition, and health benefits of barley. Finally, the reference section includes a list of barley suppliers, a scientific bibliography, and other useful information.

After trying a few of the recipes, we're sure you'll agree that *Barley is Better!*

Rosemary K. Newman, PhD   *Clarence W. (Walt) Newman, PhD*

ACKNOWLEDGEMENTS

This book is the culmination of our collective years of study, research and application on barley as a food grain. We are grateful to Montana State University for providing the resources to conduct our research, and the support of the Montana Wheat and Barley Committee for funding a good portion of our work.

Carrie Miller has provided invaluable assistance in preparing the manuscript, including recipe formatting and nutritional analysis using *Food Processor* by Esha. Our thanks also to Tanya Schultz, R.H.N., for the development and testing of the vegan recipes.

Our late daughter, Jean Johnston, was an inspiration in recipe development, with her culinary skills and artistic talent.

We are grateful for the efforts by numerous former students and co-workers, including Donna Soderberg, April Barnes, Petrea Hofer, Mary Meier, Cathy Johnson, Toots Taszut, Connie Brendan, Alan Danielson, Ted Mori, Linji Wang, Qi Xue, Milana Lazetich, Jill Abbott, Irene Eidet, Kari Hecker, Xian Han and lastly, in loving memory of Ginger Martinez.

We are also grateful to colleagues Bob Eslick, Ken Goering, Dan Biggerstaff, Dale Clark, Charles McGuire, Hadden Graham, Jim Fadel, and Sam Rao.

We also want to thank the Idaho, Oregon, and Washington Barley Commissions, Montana Grain Growers, ConAgra Mills, Abbott Laboratories, Grain Millers, Inc. and Phoenix Seed, Inc. for their invaluable support to our research. We apologize if we have overlooked any supporters.

We compliment Alberta Barley and authors Inglis and Wentworth of *Go Barley*, Torchwood Editions, Canada. It demonstrated to us that "it can be done".

Finally, we wish to thank Rebecca Soulé for the recipe photography, and Erik Petersen and the Bozeman Daily Chronicle for the barley field photography used throughout the book.

FOREWORD

The world of nutrition and health has often suffered from misinformation, poor science, and cultism. In some cases our modern dietary practices, already somewhat marginal, have been further led astray by the appearance of one or more of the latest and greatest "health food discoveries".

As a society we seem to enjoy endorsing these options with the hope that they will bring immediate improvements to our health and well-being. We forget that nutritional health is a long-term proposition and does not lend itself to instant gratification. We have a long history of abandoning an established food item in favor of something new, exciting, and nearly mystical.

The Doctors Newman, in **Barley is Better**, have taken a major step in reintroducing us to one of the oldest, best and most compatible foods. Barley may well be the most versatile grain on the planet. Barley as a human food source dates back over 10,000 years, a match for wheat, rye, or any other recorded cereal.

(It should be pointed out that in what may be the world's first athlete endorsement arrangement, the gladiators of Rome considered barley to be an essential pre-combat food and were given half a helmet of barley porridge prior to entering the arena. Those men really liked their barley.)

Cereal grains as a food group have long been recognized as a key element to health and wellness. While each has unique characteristics, barley occupies the top spot for nutritional composition and dietary versatility. The nutritional profile of barley is such that it not only meets basic needs for macro and micro nutrients, but it also acts as a major source of β-glucans and other soluble fibers.

This blend of components has been related to diabetes control, cardio-vascular status, improved large bowel health and better appetite control. In May 2005, the FDA finalized a ruling that foods containing barley could make the claim that they reduce coronary heart disease. Yes, the other cereals provide some of these outcomes, but to this observer, the advantage goes to barley.

The versatility of barley as a recipe ingredient has long been overlooked. The grain can be supplied in multiple forms including whole kernel, hull-less, flaked, grits, flour, and even quick-cooked in the form of pearl barley.

These characteristics make barley extremely flexible in food preparation. The authors make this adaptability very clear in a multitude of food types. As the reader peruses the recipe options it will be noted that there is an astonishing variety of applications to meet every taste and appetite.

This book makes a very convincing argument that "Barley is Better!"

Arthur L. Hecker, PhD
VP for R&D/Scientific Affairs
Ross Products Division, Abbott Laboratories, Chicago IL (retired)

WORKING WITH BARLEY

As with most cereal grains, the natural oils contained in barley have a tendency to oxidize when exposed to air at room temperature. This process results in what is commonly known as rancidity, meaning the product smells strong and has an off flavor. This is particularly true of whole grain products, which contain the germ. The best ways to prevent rancidity are to keep the product in an air-tight covered container and refrigerate or freeze it.

The cooking process for barley kernels consists of absorption of liquid into the kernels and changing the starch to a more digestible form. The grain kernels swell and soften in the process. In the case of flour or ground barley, the process is the same, but occurs more rapidly. Usually, the amount of water or other liquid required is double the volume of the dry grain. In other words, 1 cup of grain will require approximately 2 cups of liquid.

The general procedure is to stir barley into boiling water in a saucepan, add a pinch of salt if desired, reduce heat, cover, and allow to simmer for the specified time, stirring occasionally. Guidelines for barley-water mixtures are suggested in the following table.

Type	Barley		Water		Minutes	Yield	
Pearl	120 mL	½ cup	300 mL	1¼ cup	35	300 mL	1½ cup
Quick	120 mL	½ cup	240 mL	1 cup	10–12	300 mL	1½ cup
S.Flake	80 mL	⅓ cup	160 mL	⅔ cup	1–2*	180 mL	¾ cup
L.Flake	120 mL	½ cup	300 mL	1¼ cup	18–20	300 mL	1¼ cup
Steel-Cut	60 mL	¼ cup	240 mL	1 cup	35	240 mL	1 cup
Hulless	80 mL	⅓ cup	240 mL	1 cup	5**	150 mL	⅝ cup

*Then cover and stand 3 minutes   ** Then cover and stand 1 to 2 hours*

Whole Grain, Hulless Barley

This product is the highest in protein and dietary fiber, and has a distinctly nutty flavor and chewy texture. This is a great addition to salads, soups or casseroles. To cook whole grain barley, rinse it in a colander first, and place one cupful in a saucepan with 720 mL 2½ cups of water. If the barley is a high-β-glucan (waxy) variety, it may take more water. Boil for 5 minutes, cover and set aside for 1–2 hours, until the grain is soft. Add salt to taste or as desired. Refrigerate for storage if not used soon after these preparation steps.

Look for whole grain hulless barley in the specialty section of grocery stores, or see Suppliers of Barley Products on page 372.

Pearl Barley

When barley is pearled, the outer portion of the kernel (hull, bran, and germ) is removed. Most pearl barley products have 30–35% of the kernel removed in the process. This is one of the oldest and the most familiar type of barley available. There are many dishes that can be prepared with pearl barley that are effective in cholesterol control. The major loss in pearling is protein and oil from the germ and bran, and of course the inedible hull from covered barley. There are societies, particularly in Asia, where all barley, covered and hulless, are pearled prior to cooking. This produces a "whiter" product desired by the area consumers, but this does reduce the nutritional value. Although there is the loss of protein and oils, the remainder of the kernel (the endosperm) is a concentrated source of starch, protein and the soluble dietary fibers, beta-glucan and arabinoxylan. Pearl barley is readily available in grocery stores, usually found in or near the sections where rice, beans, and pasta are displayed.

To cook pearl barley, place the grain in a pan with double its quantity of water. Add salt if desired. Bring to a boil, reduce heat and cover. Simmer for 30–45 minutes or until tender. Add more water if barley appears dry. Cooked pearl barley can be refrigerated or frozen for later use, saving time in recipe preparation. An alternative that saves time is quick-cooking barley.

Quick-Cooking Barley

This is pearl barley that has been partially cooked and dried. Quick-cooking barley can be used in a myriad of ways. It can be substituted for regular pearl barley, particularly when a shorter cooking time is desired. When cooked half-and-half with white rice, the barley contributes to flavor as well as increasing the soluble fiber. Quick-cooking barley can also be added to soups and stews. Don't add at the start of the heating process, because quick-cooking barley is already partially cooked. You may need to experiment when substituting quick-cooking barley for pearl barley in a recipe.

Flaked Barley

Barley flakes resemble rolled oats, and are made in the same way, by steam-rolling and drying. They are available in different sized flakes. The larger, coarse flakes will require slightly longer cooking time than the finer flakes. Alone or mixed half and half with rolled oats, barley flakes make a delicious hot cereal for breakfast. Barley flakes can be used in any way you would use rolled oats, from cooked cereal to cookies to meat loaf and casseroles. This is another easy way to increase soluble fiber in the diet.

Barley Grits

This form of barley, sometimes called steel-cut barley, is a little hard to find, but is worth the search because it is so unique. Barley grits are similar to bulgur wheat, a coarse, parboiled crunchy grain. Barley grits are perfect for tabouli or other salads, also for adding texture to baked products such as bread or rolls.

Barley Flour

Barley flour is usually available in the specialty grains sections of grocery stores or in health food stores. You can make breads, pastry, cookies, muffins and cakes, substituting barley for regular wheat flour in any recipe that uses chemical leavening, such as baking powder or baking soda. For yeast breads, use no more than one-fourth of the total flour as barley flour. This is because barley lacks the stretchy gluten of wheat, so yeast bread with not rise as well with a larger percentage of barley flour. Also, barley flour has a strong tendency to absorb water, so when substituting barley flour in your own recipes, the mixture will tend to appear drier. Add a small amount of extra liquid if this happens.

Barley flour makes an excellent thickener for soups, stews, gravies and sauces. Although not as smooth as refined wheat flour, barley flour thickens very well, while adding flavor and nutrients. The type of fiber in barley makes it beneficially effective as a thickener.

USING THE RECIPES

The recipes in this book have come from many sources. Some of them are traditional recipes, given to the authors by people from various cultures. Others are old favorites that have been re-worked to use barley.

The recipes have been designed for healthy eating. For example, canola oil and canola margarine are specified, because of their desirable fatty acid composition. (Other polyunsaturated oils can be substituted if desired.) In a few instances, a small amount of butter is included for flavor. Lean meats are favored, and vegetables are prominent.

Although the recipes are not necessarily low-calorie, you always have the option of reducing portion sizes. Remember, moderation is always the key!

Finding a Recipe

First, use the main table of contents on page 5 to find the category you want and turn to that page. Now you can either use the simple recipe list to pick a recipe by name, or flip to the next page to use the detailed list, which shows the type of barley needed, preparation time, and nutritional information for each recipe.

Reading the Nutritional Information

In the detailed recipe list, you'll see nutritional information for each recipe, presented like this:

Calories	Balance			g	g	g	g	mg
	F	P	C	Fat	Prot	Carb	Fiber	Chol
510	·	·	◉	4	17	102	10 ●	5 -

The calorie bar shows the total amount of energy in one serving of the recipe, compared to all other recipes in the book.

The bubbles for fat (F), protein (P), and carbohydrate (C) show the balance of the macronutrients. You can use these bubbles to quickly find, for example, a low-fat dish, or a high-protein dish. Similarly, the bubbles for fiber and cholesterol can help you to quickly find a high-fiber or low-cholesterol dish. Numerical values are given for all nutrients as well.

Making a Recipe

The list of **ingredients** is given in US units and in metric units. To make the non-vegan version of a recipe, just use the ingredients listed in the left-hand column and ignore the right-hand column.

The list of **implements** helps you prepare your tools before you start. If you see something like "mixing bowl ×2", it usually means you'll be using both of those bowls at the same time, so we don't recommend trying to wash a single bowl and re-use it.

The **directions** are grouped into steps to help you follow along more easily. If you see an instruction labelled **Vegan:** or **Non-Vegan:**, follow it or skip it as appropriate.

The total **preparation time** is given at the start of the directions.

In some recipes, you'll see a clock symbol in the directions, like this:

This means you won't be doing anything for a while (not even stirring), so you can take care of other tasks like setting the table or preparing a side dish. But please don't leave your stove or oven unattended!

After the directions, you'll see the **yield** of the recipe and any instructions for **storage**. If storing the recipe requires a special container, it'll be listed in the list of implements.

Finally, some recipes end with **suggestions**. You can ignore these the first time you make the recipe. Once you're familiar with the recipe, you can use the suggestions to try new flavor variations or pair the recipe with other dishes.

About the Vegan Recipes

To figure out if a recipe is **vegan-friendly**, look for a **v** beside the name in the table of contents. Or, look for this symbol on the recipe page:

Some of the vegan recipes are made by substituting one ingredient for another in the same quantity, like this:

INGREDIENTS			VEGAN
80 mL	⅓ cup	**honey**	**brown rice syrup**

Other recipes will ask you to substitute different amounts, or several ingredients in place of one, like this:

INGREDIENTS			VEGAN
720 mL	3 cups	**buttermilk**	
	or...	720 mL	3 cups **soy milk**
		+ 15 mL	3 tsp **apple cider vinegar**

In a few cases, showing the vegan and non-vegan recipes on the same page would have made them too difficult to read. In those cases, the vegan recipe is always given on the next page.

In the directions, if you see an instruction labelled **Vegan:** or **Non-Vegan:**, follow it or skip it as appropriate.

Some recipes use special preparations, such as flax eggs, that you can make ahead of time. For instructions on preparing these ingredients, and for general information about buying, storing, and handling vegan ingredients, see the *Guide to Vegan Ingredients* starting on page 361.

The individual recipes will also give this page reference any time a special preparation (such as flax eggs) are used in the recipe.

BREAKFAST

Cereal, Granola, and Muesli

Pancakes, Crepes, and Waffles

pictured: Crepes, page 36

Eggs and Meat

Sweet Breakfasts

⚊ BREAKFAST

Cereal, Granola, and Muesli		Time	Barley
20 v	Barley Pecan Granola	1:10	fine flakes
22 v	Nugget Cereal	2:45	flour
24 v	Swedish Cold Cereal	:55	flakes
25 v	Muesli	:30	flakes
26 v	Swiss Hot Cereal	:40	pearl
27 v	Breakfast Barley	1:15	pearl
28 v	Baked Grains Cereal	1:50	pearl
30 v	Oat and Barley Hot Cereal	:30	flakes

Pancakes, Crepes, and Waffles

31 v	Barley Yogurt Pancakes	:50	flour
32 v	Oat and Barley Pancakes	:20	flour
33 v	Barley Wheat Pancakes	1:25	flour
34 v	Sourdough Buckwheat Pancakes	:20	flour
36 v	Crepes	:30	flakes
38 v	Multigrain Waffles	:35	flour
40	Cottage Cheese Waffles	:25	flour

Eggs and Meat

42	Barley Vegetable Cheese Omelet	:32	flakes
44 v	Scrambled Eggs, Ham, and Barley	:27	flakes
46	Barley Breakfast Sandwiches	:40	flakes
48	Sausage Brunch Casserole	1:00	quick

Sweet Breakfasts

50 v	Breakfast Blueberry Casserole	:50	flakes
54	Apple Breakfast Cake	:55	flour
56 v	Fresh Fruit Smoothie	:15	flour

Calories		Balance F	P	C	g Fat	g Prot	g Carb	g Fiber	mg Chol
590					30	12	79	12	0 -
540					3	15	117	11	5 -
440					14	12	69	13	0 -
400					5	12	83	13	0 -
350					11	10	54	11	0 -
280					6	7	51	11	0 -
560					13	11	104	10	0 -
190					2	6	38	5	5 ·
290					11	11	39	4	95
260					12	10	29	3	100
250					9	9	35	4	50
510					4	17	102	10	5 -
370					26	11	25	2	190
250					8	9	40	4	64
310					20	16	16	2	190
500					41	20	15	41	375
420					29	28	14	2	405
540					32	20	48	7	130
270					10	20	24	4	125
290					15	11	30	3	155
310					8	7	58	5	140
140					2	6	26	1	5 ·

BARLEY PECAN GRANOLA

This granola is simple, with no added fruits or seeds, but very versatile.
Great as a topping for yogurt.

INGREDIENTS

VEGAN

80 mL	⅓ cup	canola oil	
80 mL	⅓ cup	honey	brown rice syrup
10 mL	2 tsp	vanilla	
2 mL	½ tsp	salt	
1200 mL	5 cups	fine barley flakes	
300 mL	1¼ cups	coarsely ground pecans	
5 mL	1 tsp	cinnamon	

IMPLEMENTS

Oven • Stove • Small saucepan • Large mixing bowl
Baking pan, greased, 9"x13" (23x33 cm) • Airtight container (for storage)

DIRECTIONS

1:10

❶ Preheat the oven to 350°F (175°C). **Vegan:** *preheat to 200°F (95°C).*

❷ In a small saucepan, heat the honey *(or brown rice syrup)* with the oil.
Remove the saucepan from the heat.
Add the vanilla and salt to the saucepan and stir everything together.

❸ In a large bowl, combine the barley and the nuts.
Add the saucepan mixture and cinnamon to the bowl and stir thoroughly.

❹ Transfer the granola from the bowl into the greased baking pan.
Bake for 30 minutes, stirring occasionally.

❺ Turn off the oven, leaving the pan in the oven for another 20–30 minutes.
Remove the pan from the oven and let the granola cool.

Yields 6 servings. Store the granola in an airtight container.

ⓥ 〰 NUGGET CEREAL

This cereal is worth the work. The crunchy nuggets keep well in storage and are versatile for use as a topping on ice cream, yogurt or puddings.

INGREDIENTS   *VEGAN*

1440 mL	6 cups	**barley flour**
1440 mL	6 cups	**whole wheat flour**
10 mL	2 tsp	**salt**
15 mL	3 tsp	**baking soda**
600 mL	2 cups	**brown sugar**
720 mL	3 cups	**buttermilk**

		or...	720 mL	3 cups	**soy milk**
			+ 15 mL	3 tsp	**apple cider vinegar**

360 mL	1½ cups	**water**
10 mL	2 tsp	**vanilla**

IMPLEMENTS

Oven • Baking sheet, 10"x15"x2" (25x38x5 cm) • Non-stick spray
Large bowl • Small bowl • Rubber spatula • Cooling rack • Towel
Sealable plastic bags (for storage)

DIRECTIONS   2:45

❶ Preheat the oven to 300°F (150°C).

❷ In a large bowl, combine the barley flour, wheat flour, salt, and baking soda.

❸ In a smaller bowl, combine the water, vanilla, brown sugar, and buttermilk *(or soy milk and apple cider vinegar)*.

❹ Add the buttermilk mixture to the flour mixture.
Stir until the batter becomes stiff.

❺ Spray the baking sheet with non-stick spray.
Spread the batter into the baking sheet and level the top using a spatula.

6 Bake at 300°F (150°C) for 90 minutes.

🕐   *... after 90 minutes ...*

7 Move the slab of cereal from the baking sheet to a cooling rack.
Cover it with a towel and let it cool.

8 Break the cereal into small pieces.
Grate or grind the pieces into coarse crumbs or nuggets.
Spread a thin layer of the cereal on the baking sheet.

9 Bake at 250°F (120°C), stirring every 15 minutes, for 45 minutes or until the
cereal is dry and medium-brown.

10 Remove the cereal from the oven and let it cool.

Yields 15 servings. Store in a cool, dry place in sealed plastic bags.

SUGGESTIONS

Molasses can be used in place of part of the brown sugar.
You can vary the texture of the cereal by varying the size of the nuggets.

SWEDISH COLD CEREAL

You can substitute ingredients according to availability and your tastes. The important thing is having a variety of grains, nuts, and fruit.

INGREDIENTS

480 mL	2 cups	**barley flakes**
240 mL	1 cup	**four-grain hot cereal**
120 mL	½ cup	**wheat germ**
60 mL	¼ cup	**flax seeds**
240 mL	1 cup	**coconut**
240 mL	1 cup	**almonds, chopped**
120 mL	½ cup	**brown sugar**
10 mL	2 tsp	**vanilla**
120 mL	½ cup	**sunflower seeds**
120 mL	½ cup	**bran** *or 1 cup (240mL) of bran cereal*
240 mL	1 cup	**dried apples, chopped**
240 mL	1 cup	**raisins**

IMPLEMENTS

Oven • Large bowl • Baking pan, 9"x9"x11½" (23x23x29 cm)
Covered container (for storage)

DIRECTIONS   :55

❶ Preheat the oven to 275°F (135°C).

❷ In a large bowl, combine all the ingredients, except the raisins and apples.

❸ Place the mixture in a pan and bake at 275°F (135°C) for 40 minutes.

🕐   *... after 40 minutes ...*

❹ Stir in the dried apples and bake for another 40 minutes, mixing every 10.

❺ Remove the cereal from the oven and let it cool.
Fold in the raisins.

Yields 10 servings. Store in a tightly covered container.

MUESLI

The word muesli is derived from an old English word *mus*, which means "fibrous". You can find cracked wheat and rye flakes in most health food stores, or you can substitute any flaky cereal in their place.

INGREDIENTS

Muesli mix...

480 mL	2 cups	**rolled oats**
480 mL	2 cups	**barley flakes**
360 mL	1½ cups	**cracked wheat**
480 mL	2 cups	**rye flakes**
120 mL	½ cup	**almond slices**
240 mL	1 cup	**raisins**
240 mL	1 cup	**dates**, chopped
120 mL	½ cup	**wheat bran**
360 mL	1½ cups	**dried banana chips**

When preparing hot muesli...

480 mL	2 cups	water
½ mL	⅛ tsp	salt

IMPLEMENTS

Stove • Saucepan • Airtight container (for storage)

DIRECTIONS   :30

❶ Mix together the muesli mix and store it in an airtight container.

❷ In a saucepan, boil 1 cup (240 mL) of muesli mixture in the water and salt.

❸ Simmer for 10 minutes. The consistency should resemble cooked oatmeal.

Yields 12 servings.

SUGGESTIONS

Instead of boiling, try toasting this recipe in the oven to use as granola.

SWISS HOT CEREAL

A hot start to the day with a hint of sesame.

INGREDIENTS

240 mL	1 cup	**pearl barley**
15 mL	1 tbsp	**canola oil**
60 mL	¼ cup	**sesame seeds**
60 mL	¼ cup	**wheat germ**
60 mL	¼ cup	**coconut**
60 mL	¼ cup	**raisins**
1 mL	¼ tsp	**salt**
720 mL	2½ cups	**water**

IMPLEMENTS

Stove • Blender or food processor • Heavy frying pan

DIRECTIONS   :40

1. Blend the barley in a blender or food processor.

2. Heat the oil in a heavy frying pan.
   Add the barley, sesame seeds, wheat germ and coconut.
   Sauté until light brown.

3. Add the water, salt and raisins.
   Cover and steam for about 25 minutes, or until the barley is fluffy.

4. Serve hot.

Yields 4 servings.

SUGGESTIONS

For a sweeter taste, serve with milk and honey, or with brown sugar.
A variety of other fruits can be added instead of raisins to vary the flavor.

ⓥ 🌾 BREAKFAST BARLEY

This recipe has a touch of East Asian flavor, with sesame and spices.

INGREDIENTS

240 mL	1 cup	**pearl barley**
480 mL	2 cups	**water**
½ mL	⅛ tsp	**salt**
5 mL	1 tsp	**sesame oil**
3 mL	½ tsp	**cumin**
3 mL	½ tsp	**ground coriander**
60 mL	¼ cup	**golden raisins**
60 mL	¼ cup	**dried apricots**, chopped
60 mL	¼ cup	**dates**, chopped
120 mL	½ cup	**almonds**, roasted and chopped

IMPLEMENTS

Stove • Saucepan • Medium skillet

DIRECTIONS   1:15

❶ In a saucepan, combine the water, barley, and salt.
Bring to a boil.
Cover and simmer for 40 minutes.

❷ In a medium skillet, sauté the cumin and coriander in the sesame oil.
Add the raisins, apricots, and dates to the sautéed spices.
Cover and simmer for 5 minutes.

❸ Add the sautéed fruits to the cooked barley and heat thoroughly.
Stir in the nuts.

Yields 4 servings.

SUGGESTIONS

For a more European taste, leave out the sesame oil, cumin, and coriander.

BAKED GRAINS CEREAL

The time spent is worthwhile for this high-fiber, keep-for-later cereal.

INGREDIENTS

1920 mL	8 cups	water
120 mL	½ cup	wild rice
120 mL	½ cup	pearl barley
120 mL	½ cup	oatmeal
120 mL	½ cup	quinoa
120 mL	½ cup	dried mango, diced
120 mL	½ cup	pitted dated, diced
90 mL	6 tbsp	dark brown sugar
45 mL	3 tbsp	canola oil
4 mL	¾ tsp	salt
3 mL	½ tsp	ground cinnamon

IMPLEMENTS

Oven • Stove • Small saucepan • Ovenproof dish, 2½ quart (2.4L)
Non-stick spray • Aluminum foil

DID YOU KNOW?

There is no known enzyme produced by your digestive system that can digest the beta-glucans found in barley. However, there are many bacteria that live in a healthy digestive tract, especially in the colon, that can digest or ferment beta-glucans.

The main by-products of this fermentation are short-chain fatty acids, which have an additional benefit to the health and integrity of colon tissue cells.

DIRECTIONS   *1:50*

1. In a small saucepan, mix 2 cups (480 mL) of the water, plus the wild rice, barley, oatmeal, and quinoa.
   Bring to a boil.
   Cover and simmer for 10–12 minutes.

2. Preheat the oven to 375°F (190°C).
   Spray the ovenproof dish with non-stick cooking spray.

3. Mix the wild rice and barley with the remaining 6 cups (1440 mL) of water in the prepared dish.
   Stir in the mango, dates, brown sugar, canola oil, salt, and cinnamon.
   Cover loosely with foil.

4. Bake, stirring occasionally, for 1½ hours or until the grains are tender and the water is absorbed.

Yields 4 servings.

SUGGESTIONS

Can be made ahead of time and stored in the refrigerator.
Recipe can be doubled for a larger yield.

OAT AND BARLEY HOT CEREAL

This is a basic combinaton of two cereals, both high in soluble fiber.

INGREDIENTS   *VEGAN*

600 mL	2½ cups	**water**	
240 mL	1 cup	**milk**	**soy milk**
240 mL	1 cup	**oats**	
240 mL	1 cup	**barley flakes**	
45 mL	3 tbsp	**brown sugar**	
4 mL	¾ tsp	**ground cinnamon**	
1 mL	¼ tsp	**salt**	
120 mL	½ cup	**dried fruit** (of any kind)	

IMPLEMENTS

Stove • Large saucepan

DIRECTIONS   :30

1 In a large saucepan, combine the water and milk *(or soy milk)*.
Bring to a boil.

2 Add the oats, barley, brown sugar, cinnamon, and salt to the saucepan.
Cover and simmer for 10–12 minutes.

3 Add the dried fruit to the saucepan.
Continue to cook for another 5 minutes.

Yields 6 servings.

SUGGESTIONS

Serve with milk or cream.

Add nuts for more fibre and calories, or to vary the texture.

ⓥ 🌾 BARLEY YOGURT PANCAKES

These pancakes are a huge favorite. As with any recipe containing yeast, you should start the batter early to allow time for the yeast to develop.

INGREDIENTS   *VEGAN*

	1 packet	**instant dry yeast**	
120 mL	½ cup	**warm water** (110°F / 45°C)	
30 mL	2 tbsp	**honey** or **sugar**	*(use sugar)*
	2	**eggs**	**flax eggs** (p. 360)
240 mL	1 cup	**plain yogurt** or **buttermilk**	**non-dairy yogurt**
180 mL	¾ cup	**barley flour**	
60 mL	¼ cup	**all-purpose flour**	
30 mL	2 tbsp	**canola oil**	

IMPLEMENTS

Griddle • Small bowl ×2

DIRECTIONS   :50

❶ In a small bowl, dissolve the yeast in the warm water.
Stir in the honey or sugar and let the mixture set for 5 minutes.

❷ In another bowl, beat together the eggs *(or flax eggs)* and yogurt.
Add the yeast mixture to the egg mixture to create the batter.
Set the batter in a warm place for 30 minutes.

🕐   *... after 30 minutes ...*

❸ Stir the barley flour and the all-purpose flour into the batter.

❹ Spread the oil over a hot griddle.
Pour the batter to form pancakes.
Cook the pancakes, flipping as needed, until lightly-browned on both sides.

Yields 4 servings.

OAT AND BARLEY PANCAKES

You can't get any healthier than this: oats and barley together!

INGREDIENTS

			VEGAN
	2	**eggs**	**flax eggs** (p. 360)
240 mL	1 cup	**buttermilk**	**soy milk**
180 mL	¾ cup	**quick rolled oats**	
120 mL	½ cup	**barley flour**	
15 mL	1 tbsp	**sugar**	
30 mL	2 tbsp	**canola oil**	
6 mL	1¼ tsp	**baking powder**	
4 mL	¾ tsp	**baking soda**	

IMPLEMENTS

Griddle • Large bowl • Hand beater

DIRECTIONS   :20

❶ **Non-vegan:** Beat the eggs with a hand beater until they're foamy.
Vegan: Place the flax eggs in a large bowl.

❷ Stir in the buttermilk *(or soy milk)*, oats, barley flour, sugar, oil, baking powder, and baking soda.

❸ Spoon about 3 tbsp (45 mL) of batter on a hot, greased griddle to form each pancake.
Cook the pancakes until they're bubbly and dry around the edges.
Turn and cook the other side until the pancake is golden-brown.

Yields 4 servings.

SUGGESTIONS

Serve with your favorite syrup.

BARLEY WHEAT PANCAKES

This pancake batter needs time for the yeast to grow. Plan to start mixing it an hour ahead of baking the pancakes.

INGREDIENTS   *VEGAN*

	1 packet	**dry yeast**			
40 mL	8 tsp	**sugar**			
80 mL	⅓ cup	**dried buttermilk**			
	or...		240 mL	1 cup	**soy milk**
			+ 5 mL	1 tsp	**apple cider vinegar**
1 mL	¼ tsp	**salt**			
120 mL	½ cup	**barley flour**			
120 mL	½ cup	**whole wheat flour**			
30 mL	2 tbsp	**canola oil**			
	1	**egg**			**flax egg** (p. 360)
240 mL	1 cup	**water** or **fresh buttermilk**			*(use neither)*

IMPLEMENTS

Griddle • Mixing bowl

DIRECTIONS   1:25

❶ Thoroughly mix the yeast, sugar, buttermilk *(or soy milk and apple cider vinegar)*, salt, barley and whole wheat flour.

❷ Add the oil, egg *(or flax egg)* and water to the dry mix to create a batter.
Let the batter stand in a warm place for 1 hour.
The batter should bubble up when ready.

🕐   *... after 1 hour ...*

❸ Mix the batter well and pour onto a hot, greased griddle to make pancakes.

Yields 4 servings.

SOURDOUGH BUCKWHEAT PANCAKES

This is an old traditional German recipe. The batter was kept in a large earthenware crock pot with a pouring spout.

INGREDIENTS   *VEGAN*

480 mL	2 cups	**white flour**
	1 packet	**yeast**
240 mL	1 cup	**lukewarm water**
240 mL	1 cup	**buttermilk**

	or...	240 mL	1 cup	**soy milk**
		+ 5 mL	1 tsp	**apple cider vinegar**

2 mL	½ tsp	**salt**
30 mL	2 tbsp	**molasses**
240 mL	1 cup	**whole buckwheat flour**
240 mL	1 cup	**barley flour**
120 mL	½ cup	**boiling water**
3 mL	½ tsp	**baking soda**

IMPLEMENTS

Stove • Griddle • Mixing bowl • Large crock • Saucepan

DID YOU KNOW?

The gladiators in the Roman Empire were called *Hordearii*, meaning "barley men", because barley was a main part of their diet. The gladiators believed that barley greatly increased their stamina. Prior to competing in coliseum battles, they were reportedly given enough cooked barley porridge to fill one half of their helmet.

DIRECTIONS

1 Dissolve the yeast in the water.
Mix in the white flour to make a sponge batter.
Let the batter rise at room temperature for one day.

... after one day ...

2 In a large crock, combine the batter, buttermilk (or soy milk mixed with apple cider vinegar), salt, molasses, buckwheat flour, and barley flour.
Beat the batter well and let it stand in a warm place overnight.

... the next day ...

3 Mix the boiling water and baking soda into the batter.
Spoon the batter onto a hot greased griddle to make pancakes.

Yields 4 servings. Store leftover batter in the refrigerator.

Continue using the starter by adding the ingredients of Step 2 the night before. The batter may become very sour over time. If this happens, you can increase the baking soda to neutralize the sour taste.

SUGGESTIONS

Best served with real maple syrup.
You may add one or two cooked pancakes, torn in pieces, to the batter.

 CREPES

A light and versatile favorite.

INGREDIENTS

			VEGAN
	4	**eggs**, well-beaten	
	or... 240 mL	1 cup **soy milk**	
60 mL	¼ cup	**canola oil** or **olive oil**	
5 mL	1 tsp	**vanilla**	
2 mL	½ tsp	**salt**	
3 mL	½ tsp	**cinnamon**	
160 mL	⅔ cup	**milk**	**soy milk**
160 mL	⅔ cup	**flour**	
80 mL	⅓ cup	**barley flakes**	
30 mL	6 tsp	**canola margarine**	

IMPLEMENTS

Griddle • Rotary beater • Mixing bowl

DIRECTIONS   :30

❶ Combine the eggs *(or soy milk)* with the oil, vanilla, salt, cinnamon and milk *(or soy milk)* and beat with a rotary beater for two minutes.

❷ Add the flour and barley flakes and stir the batter until it's thin and runny.

❸ Spoon the batter onto a medium-hot greased griddle.
When the bottoms are firm, turn the crepes and place ½ tsp (2 mL) of margarine on each one, then fold it over in half and serve.

Yields 4 servings.

SUGGESTIONS

Serve with syrup or honey, or topped with fresh fruit and cream (pictured).
Try filling crepes with fruit or cheese.

⊙ 🌾 MULTIGRAIN WAFFLES

A healthy update to a traditional favorite.

INGREDIENTS   *VEGAN*

For the waffle mix...

480 mL	2 cups	**barley flour**	
480 mL	2 cups	**whole wheat flour**	
480 mL	2 cups	**all-purpose flour**	
240 mL	1 cup	**toasted wheat germ**	
240 mL	1 cup	**toasted oat bran**	
240 mL	1 cup	**buttermilk powder**	soy milk powder
45 mL	3 tbsp	**baking powder**	
10 mL	2 tsp	**baking soda**	
5 mL	1 tsp	**salt**	

For the waffles...

	2	**eggs**	flax eggs (p. 360)
30 mL	2 tbsp	**canola oil**	
30 mL	2 tbsp	**honey**	maple syrup
600 mL	2½ cups	**water**	

IMPLEMENTS

Waffle iron • Mixing bowl • Air-tight container (for storage)

DIRECTIONS   :35

❶ Mix all of the waffle mix ingredients together until well-blended.

❷ Store in an air-tight container in a cool, dry place until ready to use.

🕐   *... when ready to use ...*

❸ Mix 2 cups (480 mL) of prepared waffle mix with the eggs *(or flax eggs)*, canola oil, honey *(or maple syrup)*, and water until well-blended.

❹ Pour the batter onto a heated, lightly-greased waffle iron.
Bake until done.

Yields 6 servings total.

SUGGESTIONS

To save time, the waffles can be mixed while the waffle iron is heating.

DID YOU KNOW?

A special variety of barley called *Bere* (pronounced like 'bare') has been consumed in beer, porridge and breads (such as Scottish bannocks) for thousands of years. Today, the Bere grain is ground and processed for cooking in a water-powered mill, built in 1873, in the town of Birsay. You can buy bannocks made from Bere barley in restaurants in the Orkneys.

 COTTAGE CHEESE WAFFLES

These waffles were originally named Melt in Your Mouth! The recipe was given by Jill Abbott.

INGREDIENTS

120 mL	½ cup	**barley flour**
1 mL	¼ tsp	**salt**
240 mL	1 cup	**low-fat cream-style cottage cheese**
	4	**eggs**
60 mL	¼ cup	**canola oil**
120 mL	½ cup	**milk**
3 mL	½ tsp	**vanilla**

IMPLEMENTS

Blender • Waffle iron

DIRECTIONS   :25

1. Combine all of the ingredients in a blender.
Blend at high speed for one minute.

2. Pour the batter onto a heated and lightly-greased waffle iron.
Bake until done.

Yields 4 servings.

SUGGESTIONS

Serve with canola margarine and your favorite syrup.

BARLEY VEGETABLE CHEESE OMELET

This omelet is good for a quick supper meal, as well as for breakfast or brunch.

INGREDIENTS

60 mL	¼ cup	**barley flakes**
120 mL	½ cup	**water**
60 mL	¼ cup	**canola oil**
	2	**asparagus spears**, sliced
30 mL	2 tbsp	**scallions**, sliced
80 mL	⅓ cup	**cherry tomatoes**, halved
80 mL	⅓ cup	**green bell pepper**, diced
	4	**eggs**
30 mL	2 tbsp	**milk**
15 mL	1 tbsp	**pesto**
60 mL	¼ cup	**provolone** or **cheddar cheese**

IMPLEMENTS

Stove • Saucepan • Large skillet

DID YOU KNOW?

There are two kinds of starch in barley, *amylopectin* and *amylose*. Typical barley has 75% amylopectin and 25% amylose.

These molecules have different shapes, with amylopectin "branching" like a tree, while amylose is a long, coiled-up chain.

Waxy barley has 95–100% amylopectin. (The name is because the kernel looks waxy—there isn't actually wax in it.) *High-amylose* barley contains up to 70% amylose.

Both the waxy and high-amylose barleys contain significantly more digestible dietary fiber than typical barley.

DIRECTIONS

1 In a saucepan, bring the barley and water to a boil.
Cover, reduce heat, and simmer for 5 minutes.

2 Remove from heat, fluff the barley with a fork, and keep it warm.

3 Heat a large skillet and add 2 tbsp (30 mL) of the oil.
Sauté the asparagus, scallions and peppers for 5 minutes.
Remove the vegetables from the skillet.

4 Add the tomatoes to the vegetables and keep all of it warm.

5 Re-heat the skillet and add the remaining 2 tbsp (30 mL) of oil.

6 Beat the eggs in a bowl with the milk.
Add the barley and pesto to the eggs.

7 Pour the mixture into the warm skillet.
Cover and cook, stirring, for about 2 minutes, or until the egg is firm.

8 Place the vegetable mixture over half of the egg surface.
Place the cheese over the vegetables.

9 Cover the skillet and keep the omelet warm until the cheese is softened.
Fold the omelet in half over the filling and serve.

Yields 2 servings.

SCRAMBLED EGGS, HAM, AND BARLEY

A classic breakfast, enhanced with the texture and nutrition of barley.
For the vegan recipe, see the next page.

INGREDIENTS

30 mL	2 tbsp	**canola oil**
60 mL	¼ cup	**red bell pepper**, diced
30 mL	2 tbsp	**onion**, diced
60 mL	¼ cup	**cooked ham**, diced
	4	**eggs**
30 mL	2 tbsp	**milk** or **half-and-half cream**
1 mL	¼ tsp	**salt**
3 mL	½ tsp	**coarsely ground black pepper**
60 mL	¼ cup	**barley flakes**
60 mL	¼ cup	**salsa**

IMPLEMENTS

Stove • Large skillet

DIRECTIONS   :30

❶ In a large skillet, heat the canola oil.
Add the pepper and onion and sauté until the vegetables are tender.

❷ Add the ham and sauté for 1–2 minutes.

❸ In a small bowl, beat the eggs, milk, barley flakes, salt, and pepper.
Pour this mix over the vegetables and ham.

❹ Stir frequently until the mixture is cooked.
Serve with the salsa.

Yields 2 servings.

SCRAMBLED TOFU AND BARLEY

This recipe substitutes tofu and broth, while keeping the same seasoning as the non-vegan recipe on the previous page.

INGREDIENTS

30 mL	2 tbsp	**canola oil**
60 mL	¼ cup	**red bell pepper**, diced
30 mL	2 tbsp	**onion**, diced
175 g	6oz	**firm tofu**
60 mL	4 tbsp	**vegetable broth**
3 mL	½ tsp	**ground turmeric**
3 mL	½ tsp	**onion powder**
1 mL	¼ tsp	**salt**
3 mL	½ tsp	**coarsely ground black pepper**
60 mL	¼ cup	**barley flakes**
60 mL	¼ cup	**salsa**

IMPLEMENTS

Stove • Large skillet

DIRECTIONS   :30

❶ In a large skillet, heat the canola oil.
Add the pepper and onion and sauté until the vegetables are tender.

❷ Crumble the tofu into the skillet with the peppers and onion.
Add the barley flakes to the skillet.
Add 1 tbsp (15mL) of the vegetable broth.
Add the turmeric, onion powder, salt, and pepper.
Add the remaining broth 1 tbsp (15mL) at a time, until it's absorbed.

❸ Stir frequently until the mixture is cooked.
Serve with the salsa.

Yields 2 servings.

 BARLEY BREAKFAST SANDWICHES

A complete bacon-and-egg breakfast you can hold in your hand.

INGREDIENTS

	2 slices	**whole grain flat bread** or **pita bread**
	2 strips	**bacon**
	2	**eggs**
30 mL	2 tbsp	**milk**
1 mL	¼ tsp	**black pepper**
60 mL	¼ cup	**barley flakes**
60 mL	¼ cup	**cheddar cheese**, grated
30 mL	2 tbsp	**canola oil**
60 mL	¼ cup	**white mushrooms**, sliced
30 mL	2 tbsp	**scallions**, sliced
30 mL	2 tbsp	**red bell pepper**, chopped

IMPLEMENTS

Stove • Large skillet • Paper towels • Small bowl

DID YOU KNOW?

There are two distinct types of barley, *winter* and *spring*, named according to the growing season they are adapted to. Most barleys grown in the northern United States and Canada are spring barleys, while winter barleys are grown in southern areas such as Arizona and California.

DIRECTIONS   :40

1 Warm the bread, cut it into 4 half-slices, and keep it warm.

2 In a large skillet, brown the bacon until it's crisp.
Remove the bacon and wrap it in a paper towel.
Wipe the bacon grease out of the skillet.

3 In a small bowl, beat the eggs with the milk and pepper.
Add the barley flakes and set the egg mixture aside while preparing the vegetables.

4 Heat the oil in the skillet.
Sauté the mushrooms, scallions and red pepper until tender.

5 Add the egg mixture to the skillet and stir until the eggs are firm.

6 Place the egg mixture on two of the half-slices of bread.
Top the egg mixture with the cheese and a strip of bacon.
Close the sandwiches with the remaining half-slices of bread.

Yields 2 servings.

SUGGESTIONS

In a rush? Leave out the bacon and vegetables to save time.

SAUSAGE BRUNCH CASSEROLE

This is a hot dish, good for family meals or to take to a potluck.

INGREDIENTS

170g	6 oz	**ground pork sausage**
	3	**eggs**
120 mL	½ cup	**milk**
5 mL	1 tsp	**Dijon mustard**
	5 slices	**bread**, cubed
120 mL	½ cup	**quick barley**
240 mL	1 cup	**cheddar cheese**, grated

IMPLEMENTS

Oven • Stove • Large skillet • Paper towels • Small bowl • Whisk
Baking dish, 13"x9" (33x23 cm)

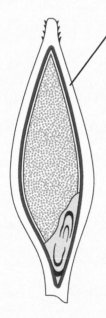

DID YOU KNOW?

The inedible outer covering of the barley kernel is called the *hull*. It protects the inner kernel from insects, disease, and weather. The hull is made mostly of cellulose, which is an indigestible fiber, along with small amounts of lignin, silicon, and other minerals.

There are two types of barley hull, *covered* and *naked*. A single gene in the plant's DNA controls the hull type. Covered barley grains have a thick, tough hull that is strongly attached to the inner kernel. Naked barley, also called hull-less, actually has a hull as well, but it is not cemented to the inner kernel.

Because the hull of the barley grain is inedible, it must either be removed at harvesting time by mechanical means (pearling), or genetically suppressed using plant breeding techniques.

DIRECTIONS

1. Preheat the oven to 350°F (175°C).

2. In a large skillet, over medium-high heat, cook the ground sausage until it's well-done.

3. Drain the ground sausage and and blot it with paper towels.

4. In a bowl, beat the eggs, milk, and mustard with a whisk until blended.
   Add the bread cubes and barley, stirring until they're well-coated.

5. Stir the sausage and ½ cup (120 mL) of the cheese into the egg mixture.

6. Pour the mixture into a greased baking dish.
   Sprinkle the remaining cheese over the top of the mixture.

7. Bake for 40–45 minutes, or until an inserted knife comes out clean.

8. Let the casserole stand for 10 minutes before cutting into squares.

Yields 6 servings.

BREAKFAST BLUEBERRY CASSEROLE

This tasty dish is great for brunches. Note that most of the preparation is done the night before. *(For the vegan recipe, turn the page.)*

INGREDIENTS

	4 slices	**whole grain bread**, day-old, cut into ½-inch cubes
120 mL	½ cup	**barley flakes**
240 mL	1 cup	**fresh or frozen blueberries**
170 g	6 oz	**cream cheese**
	4	**eggs**
120 mL	½ cup	**plain yogurt**
5 mL	1 tsp	**vanilla**
3 mL	½ tsp	**cinnamon**
120 mL	½ cup	**milk**
60 mL	¼ cup	**maple syrup**

IMPLEMENTS

Oven • Baking dish, shallow, 3 quart (2.8L) • Large bowl

DID YOU KNOW?

A single barley kernel weighs about 45 mg (about $1/500$ of an ounce). It contains all of the necessary chemical compounds and genetic information to produce a new barley plant. Fortunately for humans, there are more than enough seeds to produce the next generation of plants while leaving plenty for brewing, human food, and livestock feed.

DIRECTIONS

1. Place half of the bread cubes and barley flakes in a greased baking dish to form the base of the casserole.
Sprinkle the blueberries over the bread and barley.

2. In a large bowl, beat the cream cheese until smooth.

3. Beat the eggs, yogurt, vanilla and cinnamon into the cream cheese.
Gradually add the milk and the syrup, then blend.

4. Pour ½ of the mixture over the casserole.

5. Top the casserole with the remaining bread cubes and barley.
Cover with the remaining cream cheese mixture.

6. Cover the baking dish and refrigerate it overnight.

🕐   *... the next day ...*

7. Remove the baking dish from the refrigerator 30 minutes before baking.

8. Bake at 350°F (175°C) for 30 minutes with the cover on.

9. Uncover and bake another 20–25 minutes, or until the center is cooked thoroughly.

Yields 6 servings.

SUGGESTIONS

During the uncovered baking, additional fresh blueberries can be sprinkled over the top.

ⓥ 🌾 BREAKFAST BLUEBERRY CASSEROLE

This tasty dish is great for brunches. Note that most of the preparation is done the night before. *(For the non-vegan recipe, turn back one page.)*

INGREDIENTS

	4 slices	**whole grain bread**, day-old, cut into ½-inch cubes
120 mL	½ cup	**barley flakes**
240 mL	1 cup	**fresh or frozen blueberries**
	4	**flax eggs** (p. 360)
120 mL	½ cup	**non-dairy yogurt**
5 mL	1 tsp	**vanilla**
3 mL	½ tsp	**cinnamon**
120 mL	½ cup	**soy milk**
60 mL	¼ cup	**maple syrup**
180 mL	¾ cup	**raw cashews**, soaked in very hot water for 1 hour
5 mL	1 tsp	**lemon juice**
5 mL	1 tsp	**apple cider vinegar**
1 mL	¼ tsp	**salt**

IMPLEMENTS

Oven • Baking dish, shallow, 3 quart (2.8L) • Large bowl

DIRECTIONS

1. Drain the cashews after soaking.

2. Blend the cashews in a large bowl with the lemon juice, vinegar, and salt until completely smooth. Add tiny splashes of water if necessary.

3. Place half of the bread cubes and barley flakes in a greased baking dish to form the base of the casserole.
Sprinkle the blueberries over the bread and barley.

4. Beat the flax eggs, yogurt, vanilla and cinnamon into the cashew mixture in the large bowl.
Gradually add the soy milk and the syrup, blending.

5. Pour ½ of the mixture over the casserole.

6. Top the casserole with the remaining bread cubes and barley.
Cover with the remaining cream cheese mixture.

7. Cover the baking dish and refrigerate it overnight.

🕐 *... the next day ...*

8. Remove the baking dish from the refrigerator 30 minutes before baking.

9. Bake at 350°F (175°C) for 30 minutes with the cover on.

10. Uncover and bake another 40–45 minutes.
Allow casserole to rest for 10 minutes before serving.

Yields 6 servings.

SUGGESTIONS

During the uncovered baking, additional fresh blueberries can be sprinkled over the top.

 APPLE BREAKFAST CAKE

This dish is great for a crowd or a potluck gathering.

INGREDIENTS

	4	**apples**, tart medium-sized, peeled and sliced
180 mL	¾ cup	**dried cranberries**
90 mL	6 tbsp	**brown sugar**
5 mL	1 tsp	**ground cinnamon**
45 mL	3 tbsp	**canola margarine**
	6	**eggs**
360 mL	1½ cups	**orange juice**
240 mL	1 cup	**barley flour**
120 mL	½ cup	**wheat flour**
4 mL	¾ tsp	**salt**
30 mL	2 tbsp	**sugar**

IMPLEMENTS

Oven • Stove • Blender • Large skillet • Baking pan, 8"×8" (20×20 cm)

DID YOU KNOW?

A Swedish research group led by Professor Inger Björck showed that people with diabetes had lower blood sugar levels after eating barley bread, compared to those who ate white wheat bread.

In addition, this same group reported a carryover effect to the next meal, in which glucose levels were lower in those who ate barley at the earlier meal, even overnight.

DIRECTIONS

1. Preheat the oven to 425°F (220°C).

2. In a large skillet, sauté the apples, cranberries, brown sugar, and ¾ tsp (4 mL) of cinnamon in the margarine, until the apples begin to soften. Spread the fruit mixture in a greased baking pan.

3. In a blender, combine the eggs, orange juice, barley flour, wheat flour, and salt. Blend until smooth.

4. Pour the egg-and-flour mixture over the apples. Sprinkle with sugar and the remaining cinnamon.

5. Bake uncovered for 20–25 minutes, or until a knife inserted into the cake comes out clean.

Yields 8 servings.

SUGGESTIONS

Drizzle maple syrup over the top for an extra sweet treat!

FRESH FRUIT SMOOTHIE

Nutritious and delicious! Children love it too.

INGREDIENTS

			VEGAN
240 mL	1 cup	**plain, low-fat yogurt**	**non-dairy yogurt**
240 mL	1 cup	**1% milk**	**soy milk**
45 mL	3 tbsp	**honey**	**maple syrup**
30 mL	2 tbsp	**barley flour**	
	8	**ice cubes**	

Plus any one of the following fruits...

	8	**strawberries**
240 mL	1 cup	**raspberries**
240 mL	1 cup	**blueberries**
	1	**peach**, large
	½	**melon**, small
	1	**banana**

IMPLEMENTS

Blender

DIRECTIONS   :15

1 Combine all of the ingredients in a blender.
Whip until smooth.

Yields 4 servings.

SUGGESTIONS

Try using a mix of two fruits (using half the quantity for each) to explore new flavor combinations.

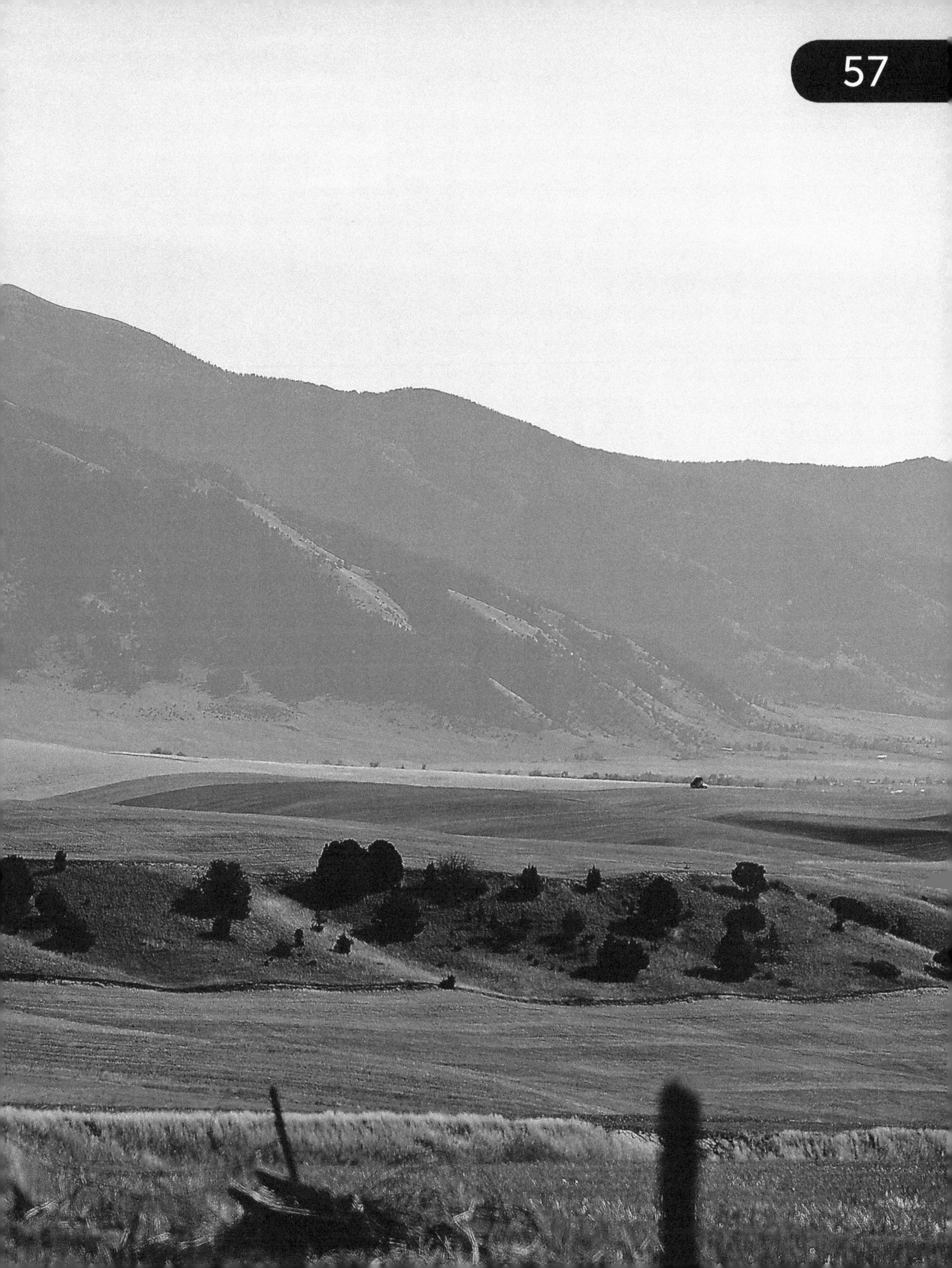

pictured: Chicken Salad, page 78

✸ SALADS ✸

ⵉ SALADS

Light Salads		Time	Barley
62 **v** Broccoli Salad		1:10	pearl
64 **v** Summer Salad		1:10	pearl
66 **v** Vegetable Salad		1:00	pearl
68 **v** Radish Salad		1:10	pearl
69 **v** Tabbouleh		1:15	grits/quick
70 **v** Pine Nut Salad		1:20	pearl
72 **v** Salsa Salad		1:05	pearl
74 **v** Fruited Barley Salad		1:15	pearl

Hearty Salads

76 Beef Salad		1:30	pearl
78 **v** Chicken Salad		1:30	pearl
82 **v** Shrimp Salad		1:05	pearl
84 **v** Corn Salad		1:00	pearl

Calories	Balance F	P	C	Fat (g)	Prot (g)	Carb (g)	Fiber (g)	Chol (mg)
220				15	6	18	6	15
210				10	4	28	6	0 -
230				9	5	37	8	0 -
95				5	1	12	2	0 -
140				12	2	8	2	0 -
190				6	4	30	7	0 -
210				11	5	24	24	20
270				9	4	46	5	0 -
480				18	48	29	7	125
450				27	19	30	6	40
310				11	17	36	6	115
160				5	3	27	4	27

ⓥ 🌾 BROCCOLI SALAD

This salad is a nutritious, tasty side dish that is welcome at potlucks too!

INGREDIENTS   *VEGAN*

120 mL	½ cup	**pearl barley**
240 mL	1 cup	**water**
½ mL	⅛ tsp	**salt**
	3	**garlic cloves**
360 mL	1½ cups	**broccoli florets**
	1	**red bell pepper**, sliced
	3	**scallions**, sliced
60 mL	¼ cup	**parsley**, minced
	8	**pitted black olives**, sliced
360 mL	1½ cups	**greens** (e.g. arugula, kale, spinach), coarsely chopped
115 g	4 oz	**feta cheese**

or...	115 g	4 oz	**firm tofu**
	45 mL	3 tbsp	**lemon juice**
	15 mL	1 tbsp	**miso paste**
	30 mL	2 tbsp	**nutritional yeast**
	2 mL	½ tsp	**salt**

Dressing...

60 mL	¼ cup	**canola oil**
5 mL	1 tsp	**cumin**
30 mL	2 tbsp	**lemon juice**
15 mL	1 tbsp	**balsamic vinegar**
1 mL	¼ tsp	**salt**
1 mL	¼ tsp	**pepper**
1 mL	¼ tsp	**oregano**
1 mL	¼ tsp	**marjoram**
1 mL	¼ tsp	**garlic**

IMPLEMENTS

Stove • Saucepan • Large bowl • Small bowl • Whisk

DIRECTIONS   *1:10*

❶ **Vegan recipe only, start with step 1:**
   Crumble tofu in a bowl.
   Add the lemon juice, miso paste, nutritional yeast, and salt.
   Mix well, taste for salt.

❷ **Both recipes, continue with step 2:**
   Combine barley, water and salt in a saucepan.
   Bring to a boil, cover and simmer 40 minutes or until tender.
   Allow to cool.

❸ In a large bowl, combine the garlic, broccoli, red pepper, scallions, parsley, olives, feta cheese *(or prepared tofu)*, and greens.

❹ In a small bowl, prepare the dressing by whisking together all of the dressing ingredients until they're well-blended.

❺ Combine the cooked barley, salad ingredients and dressing.

Yields 6 servings.

SUMMER SALAD

The vegetables can vary according to what you have on hand.

INGREDIENTS

240 mL	1 cup	**pearl barley**
480 mL	2 cups	**water**
1 mL	¼ tsp	**salt**
	3	**carrots**, shredded
180 mL	¾ cups	**celery**, chopped
	4	**radishes**, large, sliced
	3	**scallions**, with tops, thinly sliced
	1	**cucumber**, pared and sliced
	2	**tomatoes**, sliced
80 mL	⅓ cup	**canola oil**
45 mL	3 tbsp	**balsamic vinegar**
4 mL	¾ tsp	**salt**
3 mL	½ tsp	**dry mustard**
	1	**garlic clove**, minced
½ mL	⅛ tsp	**black pepper**

IMPLEMENTS

Stove • Saucepan • Large bowl • Small bowl • Whisk

DIRECTIONS   *1:10*

1. Combine the barley, water, and salt in a saucepan.
   Bring to a boil, cover, and simmer 40 minutes, or until the barley is tender.
   Set the barley aside to cool.

2. In a large bowl, mix together the carrots, celery, radishes, scallions, cucumber and tomatoes.

3. In a small bowl, whisk together the oil, vinegar, salt, mustard, garlic and black pepper.

4. Add the cooked barley to the salad ingredients and mix together.

5. Add the dressing and toss together.
   Chill until ready to serve.

Yields 8 servings.

DID YOU KNOW?

Plant foods, including cereal grains, lack some *amino acids* (especially lysine and methionine). Some human populations get most of their protein from cereal grains, but these people are usually malnourished and do not reach their maximum bodily potential.

People, especially infants and children up to 12, should combine grains with meat, milk, eggs, and fish to ensure that all essential amino acids are available.

If vegetarian, the grains should be combined with complementary plant foods to provide a balanced set of amino acids.

ⓥ 🌾 VEGETABLE SALAD

A high-fiber, healthy, and flexible salad.

INGREDIENTS

240 mL	1 cup	**pearl barley**
480 mL	2 cups	**water**
1 mL	¼ tsp	**salt**
175 mL	6 oz	**marinated artichoke hearts**
30 mL	2 tbsp	**olive oil**
15 mL	1 tbsp	**lemon juice**
	1 clove	**garlic**, finely chopped
	3	**scallions**, with tops, thinly sliced
	1	**zucchini**, small, sliced into thin half-circles
	½	**tomato**, medium, chopped
60 mL	¼ cup	**red pepper**, chopped
	1	**celery rib**, thinly sliced

IMPLEMENTS

Stove • Saucepan • Large bowl • Small bowl

DIRECTIONS

1:00

1. Combine barley, water, and salt in a saucepan.
   Bring to a boil, cover, and simmer 40 minutes, or until the barley is tender.
   Set the barley aside to cool.

2. In a small mixing bowl, slice the artichoke hearts and add the marinade from the jar.
   Add the olive oil, lemon juice, garlic and scallions to the artichokes.

3. In a large bowl, combine the zucchini, tomato, pepper, celery and barley.

4. Pour the artichoke mixture into the barley and vegetable mixture; toss them together.

5. Allow the salad to chill in the refrigerator until ready to serve.

Yields 6 servings.

SUGGESTIONS

To create different flavors, add black or green olives or vary the vegetables.

DID YOU KNOW?

Starch is a source of energy (calories). There are two types of starch in barley, with different structures. The two types are called *amylose* and *amylopectin*.

RADISH SALAD

Crispy, tasty, and very easy to make.

INGREDIENTS

120 mL	½ cup	**pearl barley**
240 mL	1 cup	**water**
½ mL	⅛ tsp	**salt**
240 mL	1 cup	**radishes**, finely chopped
	2	**celery ribs**, finely chopped
60 mL	¼ cup	**scallions**, finely chopped
480 mL	2 cups	**spinach** or **Romaine lettuce**, chopped
30 mL	2 tbsp	**balsamic vinegar dressing**
2 mL	½ tsp	**salt**
3 mL	½ tsp	**dried basil**
1 mL	¼ tsp	**pepper**

IMPLEMENTS

Stove • Small saucepan • Medium bowl • Small bowl • Whisk

DIRECTIONS
1:10

❶ In a small saucepan, combine the barley, water, and salt.
Bring to a boil, cover, and simmer 40 minutes, or until the barley is tender.
Set the barley aside to cool.

❷ In a medium bowl, combine the radishes, celery, scallions, lettuce, and pearl barley

❸ In a small bowl, whisk together the dressing, salt, basil and pepper.

❹ Add the dressing to the vegetables and mix them together.

❺ Cover and refrigerate the salad for at least 2 hours before serving.

Yields 6 servings.

ⓥ 🌾 TABBOULEH

Great for taking on camping trips.

INGREDIENTS

60 mL	¼ cup	**barley grits** or **quick-cooking barley**
120 mL	½ cup	**water**
	4	**tomatoes**, chopped
240 mL	1 cup	**parsley**, chopped
	4	**scallions**, chopped
	1	**cucumber**, diced
30 mL	2 tbsp	**fresh mint leaves**
120 mL	½ cup	**olive oil**
120 mL	½ cup	**lemon juice**
		salt and **pepper** (to taste)

IMPLEMENTS

Large bowl x2

DIRECTIONS   *1:15*

❶ Soak barley grits in water for 1 hour.

🕐   *... after 1 hour ...*

❷ Drain the barley grits and set them aside.

❸ In a large bowl, toss the tomatoes, parsley, scallions, cucumber, and mint together.

❹ Add the grits, olive oil, lemon juice, salt, and pepper.
Mix everything together.

❺ Refrigerate until chilled.

Yields 10 servings. Can be stored in the refrigerator for several days.

V ⚜ PINE NUT SALAD

A refreshing and tasty salad for any season.

INGREDIENTS   *VEGAN*

480 mL	2 cups	**chicken broth**	**vegetable broth**
240 mL	1 cup	**pearl barley**	
180 mL	¾ cup	**red bell pepper**, chopped	
240 mL	1 cup	**cucumber**, diced	
480 mL	2 cups	**Iceberg lettuce**, chopped	
15 mL	1 tbsp	**fresh dill**, chopped	
15 mL	1 tbsp	**fresh parsley**, chopped	
45 mL	3 tbsp	**lemon juice**	
30 mL	2 tbsp	**olive oil**	
4 mL	¾ tsp	**sugar**	
2 mL	½ tsp	**salt**	
2 mL	½ tsp	**pepper**	
30 mL	2 tbsp	**pine nuts**, toasted	

IMPLEMENTS

Oven • Stove • Saucepan • Large bowl • Small bowl • Whisk

DIRECTIONS   *1:20*

❶ Preheat the oven to 375°F (190°C).
Toast the pine nuts for 10 minutes, or until golden brown.
Set the pine nuts aside to cool.

❷ Combine the chicken broth and barley in a saucepan.
Bring to a boil, cover, and simmer 40 minutes, or until the barley is tender.
Set the barley aside to cool.

❸ In a large bowl, combine the barley, red pepper, cucumber, lettuce, dill, and parsley.

❹ In a small bowl, whisk together the lemon juice, olive oil, sugar, salt, and pepper.

❺ Add the dressing to the barley mixture and mix them together.

❻ Sprinkle the pine nuts over the top of the salad.

Yields 6 servings.

DID YOU KNOW?

Barley is an ancient grain. It originated as a wild grass, growing on lands near the eastern Mediterranean Sea.

SALSA SALAD

The salsa adds a bit of zing, and the water chestnuts are tasty as well as crunchy.

INGREDIENTS   *VEGAN*

120 mL	½ cup	**pearl barley**
240 mL	1 cup	**water**
½ mL	⅛ tsp	**salt**
120 mL	½ cup	**celery**, chopped
120 mL	½ cup	**scallions**, chopped
80 mL	⅓ cup	**red bell peppers**, diced
	8 oz	**sliced water chestnuts**
60 mL	¼ cup	**parsley**, chopped
120 mL	½ cup	**hot pepper cheese**, shredded

or...	3 mL	½ tsp	**red chili flakes**

120 mL	½ cup	**light mayonnaise** **vegan mayonnaise**
45 mL	3 tbsp	**salsa**
720 mL	2½ cups	**fresh spinach leaves**, shredded
80 mL	⅓ cup	**light sour cream**

or...	80 mL	⅓ cup	**raw cashews**
	5 mL	1 tsp	**lemon juice**
	5 mL	1 tsp	**apple cider vinegar**
	30 mL	2 tbsp	**water**
		pinch	**salt**

IMPLEMENTS

Stove • Small saucepan • Large bowl • Small bowl

DIRECTIONS

1 **Vegan recipe only, start with step 1:**
Soak the raw cashes in very hot water for 30 minutes then drain them.
Blend the cashews with the lemon juice, apple cider vinegar, water, and a pinch of salt until smooth.
Add more water, 1 tbsp (15 mL) at a time, to achieve a sour-cream-like consistency.

2 **Both recipes, continue with step 2:**
Combine the barley, water, and ⅛ tsp (0.5 mL) of salt in a small saucepan.
Bring to a boil and simmer for 40 minutes, or until the barley is tender.
Set the barley aside to cool.

3 In a large bowl, mix together the cooked barley, celery, scallions, bell peppers, water chestnuts, parsley, and hot pepper cheese *(or red chili flakes)*.

4 In a small bowl, combine the mayonnaise, sour cream *(or cashew cream)*, and salsa.

5 Add the dressing mix to the barley and vegetables and mix well.

6 Add the spinach leaves and mix together gently.

Yields 6 servings.

FRUITED BARLEY SALAD

Refreshing for lunch or dinner, and is a hit at potlucks. Try adding pineapple as a variation.

INGREDIENTS

VEGAN

Dressing:

45 mL	3 tbsp	**olive oil**
120 mL	½ cup	**orange juice**
30 mL	2 tbsp	**honey**

brown rice syrup

Salad:

240 mL	1 cup	**pearl barley**
480 mL	2 cups	**water**
1 mL	¼ tsp	**salt**
	2	**apples**, chopped
60 mL	¼ cup	**lemon juice**
240 mL	1 cup	**golden raisins**
240 mL	1 cup	**seedless grapes**, halved
30 mL	2 tbsp	**mint**, chopped
30 mL	2 tbsp	**parsley**, chopped
30 mL	2 tbsp	**chives**, chopped
80 mL	⅓ cup	**pecans**, chopped
		pepper, to taste

IMPLEMENTS

Stove • Large bowl • Small bowl • Whisk

DIRECTIONS   *1:15*

1 In a small bowl, whisk together the dressing ingredients, then set aside.

2 Combine the barley, water, and salt in a saucepan.
Bring to a boil, cover, and simmer 40 minutes, or until the barley is tender.
Set aside to cool.

3 In a large bowl, toss together the apples and lemon juice.
Add the raisins, grapes, mint, parsley, and chives.

4 Add the dressing to the salad and toss.
Season with pepper.
Cover and chill.

5 Top with chopped pecans before serving.

Yields 8 servings.

 BEEF SALAD

This salad is a main dish. Add crusty bread or rolls for a complete meal.

INGREDIENTS

240 mL	1 cup	**pearl barley**
480 mL	2 cups	**water**
	1	**beef-flavored bouillon cube** or **envelope**
	1	**lemon**, large
30 mL	2 tbsp	**olive oil**
5 mL	1 tsp	**salt**
1 mL	¼ tsp	**black pepper**
115 g	4 oz	**green beans**
80 mL	⅓ cup	**parsley**, chopped
60 mL	¼ cup	**mint**, chopped
	1	**scallion**, chopped
900 g	2 lbs	**beef steak**
240 mL	1 cup	**cherry tomatoes**
		mint sprigs (for garnish)

IMPLEMENTS

Oven • Stove • Saucepan • Large bowl • Grater/zester • Whisk

DID YOU KNOW?

Vitamins are divided into two groups. *Fat-soluble* vitamins include A (retinol), D (calciferol), E (alpha-tocopherol), and K (menadione). *Water-soluble* vitamins include B_1 (thiamin), B_2 (riboflavin), B_3 (pantothenic acid), B_6 (pyridoxine), B_{12} niacin (nicotinic acid), biotin, folic acid, choline, and vitamin C (ascorbic acid).

Barley kernels do not contain vitamins A, D, K, C, or B_{12}. However, barley is a good secondary source of vitamins E, B_1, B_2, and B_3.

DIRECTIONS   *1:30*

1. Combine the barley, water, and bouillon in a saucepan.
   Bring to a boil and simmer for 40 minutes.

2. In a large bowl, grate 1 tsp (5 mL) of lemon peel.
   Squeeze 3 tbsp (45 mL) of juice from the lemon into the bowl.

3. Whisk together the lemon, olive oil, salt and pepper.

4. Add the barley to the lemon mixture and mix until the barley is coated.
   Cover and chill.

5. Cut the green beans in half.
   Place the beans in a saucepan with about 1 inch (2.5 cm) of water.
   Add ½ tsp (2 mL) salt and bring the water to a boil.
   Simmer 5–10 minutes, or until the beans are tender.

6. Broil the steak to desired doneness.
   Cut the steak into strips. Set the strips aside and keep them warm.

7. Toss the chilled barley mixture, cooked green beans, parsley, mint, and
   scallion together until well-mixed.

8. Arrange the barley mixture, beef strips, and cherry tomatoes on a platter.
   Garnish with mint sprigs.

Yields 6 servings.

CHICKEN SALAD

This salad can be the centerpiece for a lunch or light supper.

INGREDIENTS   *VEGAN*

240 mL	1 cup	**pearl barley**	
480 mL	2 cups	**water**	
1 mL	¼ tsp	**salt**	
450 g	1 lb	**boneless chicken breasts**	**extra-firm tofu**
120 mL	½ cup	**dry white wine**	
5 mL	1 tsp	**lemon juice**	
480 mL	2 cups	**water**	
	or...	30 mL	2 tbsp	**olive oil**
	2 sprigs	**fresh thyme** *or...*	
1 mL	¼ tsp	**dried thyme**	
	2	**bay leaves**	
	10	**black pepper corns**	
	1	**cucumber**, large, diced	
	1	**tomato**, large, diced	
	½ bunch	**cilantro**, chopped	
	½ bunch	**parsley**, chopped	
	1 bunch	**chives**, chopped	
10 mL	2 tsp	**Dijon mustard**	
80 mL	⅓ cup	**lemon juice**	
160 mL	⅔ cup	**olive oil**	

IMPLEMENTS

Stove • Large saucepan • Saucepan • Large bowl • Small bowl • Whisk

For vegan recipe, add:
Medium Bowl • Baking sheet

recipe continues on 80 (non-vegan) or 81 (vegan) ▶

▶ **Chicken Salad,** *continued from 78.*

DIRECTIONS, NON-VEGAN   *1:30*

1. Combine the barley, water, and salt in a saucepan.
   Bring to a boil, cover, and simmer 40 minutes, or until the barley is tender.

2. In a large saucepan, combine the white wine, 1 tsp (5 mL) of lemon juice, water, thyme, bay leaves, and peppercorns.

3. Bring the white wine mix to a boil.
   Add the chicken breasts.
   Gently simmer for 15–20 minutes.

4. Remove the chicken from the saucepan and cut it into bite-sized pieces.
   Set the chicken aside to cool.

5. In a large bowl, mix the cucumber, tomato, cilantro, parsley, and chives.

6. In a small bowl, whisk together the mustard, olive oil, and the remaining ⅓ cup (80 mL) of lemon juice.

7. Add the mustard mixture to vegetables.
   Add the barley to the vegetables and mix together thoroughly.

8. Arrange the chicken pieces over the top of the salad and serve.

Yields 6 servings.

► **Chicken Salad,** *continued from 78.*

Ⓥ DIRECTIONS, VEGAN   *1:30*

❶ Combine the barley, water, and salt in a saucepan.
Bring to a boil, cover, and simmer 40 minutes, or until the barley is tender.

❷ Preheat the oven to 400°F (205°C).

❸ Whisk the white wine, 1 tsp (5 mL) of lemon juice, 2 tbsp (30 mL) of olive oil, thyme, bay leaves, and peppercorns in a medium bowl.

❹ Cut the tofu into 2"x2"x¼" (5x5x0.25 cm) slabs.
Marinate the tofu in the wine mixture for at least 30 minutes, and up to 4 hours, tossing every 15–20 minutes to ensure an even coating.

❺ Place the tofu on a baking sheet in a single layer.
Bake the tofu for 20 minutes at 400°F (205°C).

❻ In a large bowl, mix the cucumber, tomato, cilantro, parsley, and chives.

❼ In a small bowl, whisk together the mustard and the remaining ⅓ cup (80 mL) of lemon juice and ⅔ cup (160 mL) of olive oil.

❽ Add the mustard mixture to the vegetables.
Add the barley to the vegetables and mix together thoroughly.

❾ Arrange the tofu over the top of the salad and serve.

Yields 6 servings.

ⓥ 🌾 SHRIMP SALAD

This salad can be a meal in itself, either for lunch or a light supper.

INGREDIENTS   *VEGAN*

240 mL	1 cup	**pearl barley**	
480 mL	2 cups	**water**	
1 mL	¼ tsp	**salt**	
450 g	1 lb	**cooked small shrimp**	
	or... 480 mL	2 cups	**cooked cannellini beans**
240 g	8½ oz	**canned artichoke hearts**, drained and diced	
160 mL	⅔ cup	**celery**, chopped	
80 mL	⅓ cup	**scallions**, chopped	
120 mL	½ cup	**light mayonnaise**	**vegan mayonnaise**
240 mL	1 cup	**plain yogurt**	**plain soy yogurt**
2 mL	½ tsp	**dill weed**	
5 mL	1 tsp	**chives**, chopped	
		salt (to taste)	
		pepper (to taste)	
120 mL	½ cup	**light sour cream**	
	or... 120 mL	½ cup	**raw cashews**
	8mL	1½ tsp	**lemon juice**
	5mL	1 tsp	**apple cider vinegar**
	45 mL	3 tbsp	**water**
	pinch		**salt**

lettuce (to serve on)
cherry tomatoes (for garnish)
lemon slices (for garnish)

IMPLEMENTS

Stove • Saucepan • Large bowl • Small bowl

DIRECTIONS

1 **Vegan recipe only, start with step 1:**
Soak the raw cashews in very hot water for 30 minutes then drain them.
Blend the cashews with the lemon juice, apple cider vinegar, water, and a pinch of salt until smooth.
Add more water, 1 tbsp (15 mL) at a time, to achieve a sour-cream-like consistency.

2 **Both recipes, continue with step 2:**
Combine the barley, water, and ¼ tsp (1 mL) of salt in a small saucepan.
Bring to a boil, cover, and simmer 40 minutes, or until the barley is tender.
Set the barley aside to cool.

3 Combine the cooked barley, shrimp *(or cannellini beans)*, artichokes, celery and scallions in a large bowl and mix well.

4 Combine the sour cream *(or cashew cream)*, mayonnaise, yogurt, dill and chives in a small bowl.
Season with salt and pepper as desired.

5 Mix together the cream sauce and the barley mixture.
Chill before serving.

6 Serve on a bed of lettuce.
Garnish with cherry tomatoes and lemon slices.

Yields 6 servings.

CORN SALAD

A hearty salad that makes a good accompaniment to a sandwich.

INGREDIENTS

240 mL	1 cup	**pearl barley**
480 mL	2 cups	**water**
1 mL	¼ tsp	**salt**
480 mL	2 cups	**corn**
120 mL	½ cup	**red bell pepper**, chopped
120 mL	½ cup	**green bell pepper**, chopped
	3	**scallions**, chopped
15 mL	1 tbsp	**cilantro**
30 mL	2 tbsp	**lemon juice**
30 mL	2 tbsp	**canola oil**
2 mL	½ tsp	**salt**
3 mL	½ tsp	**thyme**
½ mL	⅛ tsp	**pepper**

IMPLEMENTS

Stove • Medium saucepan • Large bowl • Small bowl • Whisk

DIRECTIONS   *1:00*

1. In a medium saucepan, combine the water, barley, and salt.
   Bring to a boil and simmer for 40 minutes, or until the barley is tender.
   Set aside to cool.

2. In a small bowl, whisk the lemon juice, oil, salt, thyme, and pepper.

3. In a large bowl, combine the barley, corn, peppers, scallions and cilantro.

4. Mix the dressing into the barley and vegetables.

Yields 6 servings.

pictured: Bean-and-Butternut Stew, page 112

 SOUPS

Soups

Stews

Chilled Soups

SOUPS

Soups		Time	Barley
90 v	Traditional Beef Barley Soup	2:30	pearl
93 v	Norwegian Vegetable Soup	1:30	pearl
94 v	Vegetarian Barley Soup	1:45	pearl
96 v	Mexican Chili Soup	1:10	pearl
98 v	Chicken Soup	1:45	pearl
100 v	Cream of Mushroom Soup	1:30	pearl
102	Barley Onion Soup with Meatballs	2:05	pearl
104 v	Cream of Tomato Soup	1:35	pearl
106 v	Broccoli and Cheese Soup	1:35	pearl
107 v	Pumpkin Soup	1:00	pearl
108 v	Asparagus Soup	1:05	quick

Stews

110 v	Beef Stew	1:50	pearl
112 v	Bean-and-Butternut Stew	1:55	pearl

Chilled Soups

115 v	Chilled Fruit Soup	1:45	quick

Calories	Balance F	P	C	Fat g	Prot g	Carb g	Fiber g	Chol mg
180	·	●	●	4	9	28	7 ◉	15 •
160	●	·	●	5	7	24	5 ◉	5 •
340	●	·	●	8	8	62	8 ●	0 -
400	·	●	●	9	21	51	12 ◉	40 ●
150	●	●	·	7	6	16	3 ●	20 ●
160	●	·	●	8	4	21	4 ●	15 •
300	●	●	·	17	17	22	3 ·	60 ●
230	●	·	●	10	5	30	5 ●	20 •
190	●	●	·	8	12	18	3 ●	20 ●
210	●	·	●	10	6	27	5 ●	15 •
190	●	●	·	9	10	23	9 ◉	10 •
340	●	●	·	12	24	32	6 ●	55 ●
280	●	●	·	13	12	28	7 ◉	20 •
350	-	-	◉	1	3	87	8 ●	0 -

ⓥ 🌾 TRADITIONAL BEEF BARLEY SOUP

This soup is a changeable feast. You can substitute ingredients according to your own taste.

INGREDIENTS   *VEGAN*

225 g	8 oz	**beef chuck**, trimmed and boneless	
	or...	240 mL	1 cup	**red lentils**
240 mL	1 cup	**pearl barley**	
5 mL	1 tsp	**salt**	
3 mL	½ tsp	**pepper**	
	1	**bay leaf**	
1920 mL	8 cups	**water**	**vegetable broth**
240 mL	1 cup	**carrot**, diced	
120 mL	½ cup	**onion**, diced	
240 mL	1 cup	**turnip**, diced	
160 mL	⅔ cup	**celery**, diced	
240 mL	1 cup	**potato**, diced	
425 g	15 oz	**canned pinto beans**, or other beans	
480 mL	2 cups	**chard**, escarole, or other greens	
15 mL	1 tbsp	**soy sauce**	
15 mL	1 tbsp	**Worcestershire sauce**	**vegan Worcestershire**
10 mL	2 tsp	**parsley**	

IMPLEMENTS

Stove • Large pot

recipe continues on 92 ▶

▶ **Traditional Beef Barley Soup,** *continued from 90.*

DIRECTIONS   *2:30*

1 In a large pot, combine the beef, barley, salt, pepper, bay leaf, and water.
(Vegan recipe: don't add the lentils yet.)

2 Bring to a boil.
Reduce heat and simmer for 1½ hours, stirring occasionally.

3 Add the vegetables and pinto beans to the pot.
(Vegan recipe: add the lentils now.)
Simmer for 20 minutes.

4 Add the chard (or other greens). ·
Simmer for another 10 minutes.

5 Stir in the soy sauce and Worcestershire sauce.
Remove the pot from the heat.

6 Stir in the parsley.
Cover and let stand for 10 minutes.

Yields 10 servings.

SUGGESTIONS

You can use beef broth in place of water. If you do, consider leaving out
the salt and soy sauce.
If you have access to a beef soup-bone, you can add it at the beginning.

Ⓥ 🌾 NORWEGIAN VEGETABLE SOUP

Our Norwegian friend, Birger Svihus, made this soup while visiting at our home. He had no written recipe, just his memory and intuition. This is my best interpretation of his directions.

INGREDIENTS

			VEGAN
1920 mL	8 cups	**chicken broth**	**vegetable broth**
120 mL	½ cup	**pearl barley**	
	1	**leek**, cut up	
	1	**parsnip**, large, diced	
	1	**turnip**, medium, diced	
	2	**heads of baby bok choy**, small, chopped	
	2	**red potatoes**, diced	
5 mL	1 tsp	**garlic**, minced	
5 mL	1 tsp	**bouquet garni**	
120 mL	½ cup	**diced meat** (e.g. summer sausage, ham, frankfurters)	**crumbled tempeh**
		or...	
240 mL	1 cup	**mushrooms**, sliced	
30 mL	2 tbsp	**canola oil**	
15 mL	1 tbsp	**paprika**	

IMPLEMENTS

Stove • Large heavy pot • Skillet

DIRECTIONS   *1:30*

❶ In a large heavy pot, combine the broth, barley, leek, parsnip, turnip, bok choy, potatoes, garlic, and bouquet garni.
Bring to a boil, reduce heat, and simmer for 1 hour.

❷ Meanwhile, sauté the mushrooms in oil, until softened but not browned.

❸ Add the meat *(or tempeh)* and mushrooms to the pot.

❹ Garnish with paprika.

Yields 12 servings. This is a big batch, but it reheats well.

VEGETARIAN BARLEY SOUP

A meatless option which is good on its own. As with the traditional beef barley soup, it's a flexible recipe that you can experiment with.

INGREDIENTS

45 mL	3 tbsp	**canola oil**
340 g	12 oz	**mushrooms**, fresh
240 mL	1 cup	**onions**, chopped
	6	**carrots**, peeled and diced
	4	**parsnips**, peeled and diced
	1	**leek**, trimmed and sliced
15 mL	1 tbsp	**garlic**, minced
960 mL	4 cups	**vegetable broth**
240 mL	1 cup	**pearl barley**
10 mL	2 tsp	**thyme**
	2	**bay leaves**
120 mL	½ cup	**parsley, chopped**
		salt (as desired for taste)
		pepper (as desired for taste)

IMPLEMENTS

Stove • Non-stick skillet • Large heavy pot

DIRECTIONS   *1:45*

❶ Heat 1 tbsp (15 mL) of the oil in a non-stick skillet.
Add the mushrooms and sauté for 5 minutes.
Remove the mushrooms from the skillet and set them aside.

❷ Heat the remaining 2 tbsp (30mL) of oil in a large pot over medium heat.
Add the chopped onions.
Cook for 5 minutes, stirring.

❸ Add the carrots, parsnips, leek, and garlic to the pot.
Cook for 10 minutes, stirring occasionally.

❹ Add the vegetable broth, barley, thyme, bay leaves, salt, and pepper.

❺ Bring the mixture to a boil, reduce heat, and simmer for 1 hour, or until the barley is tender.

❻ Add the mushrooms to the pot.
Stir for 5 minutes.

❼ Fold in the parsley just before serving.

Yields 6 servings.

SUGGESTIONS
For new tastes, try adding tomatoes or other vegetables.

MEXICAN CHILI SOUP

A flavorful soup that you can season to your tastes by varying the balance of the herbs and spices.

INGREDIENTS

			VEGAN
450 g	1 pound	**ground beef**, lean	**tempeh**, crumbled
	1	**onion**, medium, chopped	
480 mL	2 cups	**water**	
410 g	14½ oz	**canned diced tomatoes**, with liquid	
440 g	15½ oz	**canned hominy**, drained	
440 g	15½ oz	**canned ranch-style beans** or **chili beans**	
450 g	16 oz	**canned kidney beans**, drained and rinsed	
115 g	4 oz	**green chilies**	
180 mL	¾ cup	**pearl barley**	
5 mL	1 tsp	**salt**	
30 mL	2 tbsp	**chili powder**	
10 mL	2 tsp	**dried oregano**	
3 mL	½ tsp	**ground cumin**	
30 mL	2 tbsp	**brown sugar**	
1 mL	¼ tsp	**cayenne pepper**	
		cheddar cheese, shredded (optional)	
	or...		*(leave out cheese)*
120 mL	½ cup	**sour cream** (optional)	

	or...	120 mL	½ cup	**raw cashews**
		8 mL	1½ tsp	**lemon juice**
		5 mL	1 tsp	**apple cider vinegar**
		3 tbsp	45 mL	**water**
			pinch	**salt**

IMPLEMENTS

Dutch oven or soup kettle

DIRECTIONS   *1:10*

1. **Vegan recipe only, start with step 1:**
   Soak the raw cashews in very hot water for 30 minutes, then drain them.
   Blend the cashews with the lemon juice, apple cider vinegar, water, and a pinch of salt, until smooth.
   Add more water, 1 tbsp (15 mL) at a time, to achieve a consistency like sour cream.

2. **Non-vegan:** In a Dutch oven or soup kettle, cook the beef and the onions over medium heat until the meat is no longer pink. Drain off the fat.

   Vegan: In a Dutch oven or soup kettle, cook the crumbled tempeh and the onions over medium heat until the onions are soft.

3. Add the water, tomatoes, hominy, beans, chilies, barley, salt, chili powder, oregano, cumin, brown sugar, and cayenne.
   Bring to a boil.

4. Reduce heat, cover, and simmer for 30 minutes.

🕐   *... after 30 minutes ...*

5. Remove the soup from the heat.
   If desired, stir in sour cream *(or cashew cream)*.
   Non-vegan: If desired, garnish with shredded cheese.

Yields 8 servings.

SUGGESTIONS
Cornbread goes well with this soup.

ⓥ 🌾 CHICKEN SOUP

This is a hearty soup with great flavor.

INGREDIENTS   *VEGAN*

30 mL	2 tbsp	**canola oil**	
120 mL	½ cup	**onions**, chopped	
	1	**leek**, chopped	
120 mL	½ cup	**carrots**, chopped	
	2 cloves	**garlic**, minced	
240 mL	1 cup	**cooked chicken**, cut up	cooked chickpeas
120 mL	½ cup	**pearl barley**	
30 mL	2 tbsp	**flour**	
1440 mL	6 cups	**chicken broth**	vegetable broth
5 mL	1 tsp	**pepper**	
5 mL	1 tsp	**thyme**	
120 mL	½ cup	**half-and-half cream** (optional)	

	or...	60 mL	¼ cup	**soy cream**
		60 mL	¼ cup	**soy milk**

60 mL	¼ cup	**parsley**, chopped	

IMPLEMENTS

Stove • Large heavy pot

DIRECTIONS   *1:45*

1 Heat the oil in a large, heavy pot.

2 Add the onions, leek, carrots, and garlic.
Sauté the vegetables until they are softened, without browning them.

3 Add the chicken (or chickpeas) and barley, then stir.
Cook gently for 2–3 minutes.

4 Add the flour and continue to stir for 1 minute.

5 Gradually add the broth, pepper, and thyme.
Bring to a boil, reduce heat and simmer for 60–90 minutes.

🕐   *... after 60–90 minutes ...*

6 Reduce the heat.
Add the half-and-half cream (or soy cream and soy milk), stirring well.
Do not let the soup come back to a boil.

7 Garnish the soup with parsley.

Yields 8 servings.

CREAM OF MUSHROOM SOUP

Great for warming up on a winter day.

INGREDIENTS   *VEGAN*

960 mL	4 cups	water	
	2	carrots, peeled and chopped	
	2	celery ribs, chopped	
240 mL	1 cup	pearl barley	
5 mL	1 tsp	salt	
30 mL	2 tbsp	butter or canola oil	*(use canola oil)*
450 g	1 pound	mushrooms, washed and coarsely chopped	
960 mL	4 cups	chicken or beef broth	vegetable broth
240 mL	1 cup	greens, coarsely chopped	
120 mL	½ cup	heavy cream	soy cream
5 mL	1 tsp	Worcestershire sauce	vegan Worcestershire
		pepper (as desired for taste)	

IMPLEMENTS

Stove • Large heavy pot • Large non-stick skillet

DID YOU KNOW?

Proteins are molecules usually formed as chains or groups of small carbon-based compounds called *amino acids*. There are about twenty different amino acids in our diet. Nine of them are classified as *essential,* because our body can't synthesize enough of them on its own, so we must get them from our food. The rest are classified as *non-essential*; our body can synthesize enough of them as long as sufficient nitrogen is available.

DIRECTIONS   *1:30*

1 In a large heavy pot, combine the water, carrots, celery, barley, and salt. Bring to a boil, reduce heat, and simmer for 30 minutes.

2 Meanwhile, in a large non-stick skillet, sauté the mushrooms in the butter or oil until the mushrooms are tender, but not browned. Do not overcook.

3 Add the mushrooms to the barley mixture. Simmer for another 15 minutes, stirring frequently.

4 Stir in the broth and the chopped greens. Return the mixture to a boil.

5 Remove the pot from the heat and stir in the heavy cream (or soy cream).

6 Season with Worcestershire sauce and pepper as desired.

Yields 10 servings. Keeps well in the refrigerator and reheats well.

SUGGESTIONS

This recipe can be halved.

BARLEY ONION SOUP WITH MEATBALLS

This soup is hearty; a meal in itself if served with bread and green salad.

INGREDIENTS

120 mL	½ cup	**pearl barley**
1920 mL	8 cups	**beef broth**
450 g	1 pound	**ground beef**, lean
5 mL	1 tsp	**salt**
3 mL	½ tsp	**pepper**
	1	**egg**
60 mL	¼ cup	**bread crumbs**
60 mL	¼ cup	**canola oil**
	3	**onions**, large, sliced
15 mL	1 tbsp	**Worcestershire sauce**
		garlic powder (as desired for taste)
		thyme (as desired for taste)

IMPLEMENTS

Stove • Large heavy pot • Bowl • Large skillet

DIRECTIONS   *2:05*

① Combine the barley and the broth in a large heavy pot.
Bring to a boil, reduce heat, and simmer for 45 minutes.

② In a bowl, combine the ground beef, egg, bread crumbs, salt, and pepper.
Blend well and form into meatballs.

③ In a large skillet, brown the meatballs in the oil, then move them to a plate
and keep them warm.

④ Add the onions to the meat drippings and stir until they're soft.

⑤ Add the onions and meatballs to the barley broth mixture.
Simmer for 20–30 minutes.

Yields 8 servings.

DID YOU KNOW?

The amino acid *lysine* is lacking from most grains. However, Dr. E.T Mertz at Purdue University identified a corn type that contains significantly more lysine than most corn. This has been extremely important in providing higher-quality protein in areas dependent on corn.

Similarly, Dr. Lars Munck of Sweden identified a barley that contains even higher levels of lysine than the high-lysine corn. At this time, the high-lysine barley has not been put to use by a human population yet.

CREAM OF TOMATO SOUP

The barley adds flavor, texture, and fiber to this tasty soup.

INGREDIENTS

			VEGAN
410 g	14.5 oz	**canned diced tomatoes**	
240 mL	1 cup	**chicken broth**	**vegetable broth**
30 mL	2 tbsp	**canola margarine**	**coconut oil**
30 mL	2 tbsp	**sugar**	
15 mL	1 tbsp	**onion**, finely chopped	
1 mL	¼ tsp	**baking soda**	
480 mL	2 cups	**half-and-half cream**	
	or...	240 mL	1 cup	**soy cream**
		240 mL	1 cup	**soy milk**
240 mL	1 cup	**pearl barley**	
5 mL	1 tsp	**dried basil leaves**	

IMPLEMENTS

Stove • Microwave or double boiler • Large heavy pot

DID YOU KNOW?

Starch and cellulose are both built from many molecules of glucose linked together. In starch, the type of links are named *alpha links*, and in cellulose they're named *beta links*. The different structure is what makes starch digestible, while cellulose is an indigestible dietary fiber.

DIRECTIONS

1. Combine the tomatoes, broth, margarine (or oil), sugar, onion, and baking soda in a large heavy pot.
Heat to boiling, reduce heat, and simmer for 30 minutes.

🕐   *... after 30 minutes ...*

2. Add the barley and continue to simmer for an additional 30 minutes.

🕐   *... after 30 minutes ...*

3. Heat the half-and-half cream (or soy cream mixed with soy milk) in a double boiler or in the microwave. Do not allow the cream to boil.

4. Add the half-and-half cream (or soy cream and soy milk) slowly to the tomato mixture while stirring constantly.

5. Sprinkle the basil over the surface of the soup.

Yields 8 servings.

BROCCOLI AND CHEESE SOUP

A classic creamy soup that's great for kids too. Goes well with crusty bread.

INGREDIENTS

			VEGAN
720 mL	2½ cups	**chicken broth**	**vegetable broth**
120 mL	½ cup	**pearl barley**	
480 mL	2 cups	**broccoli**, finely chopped	
240 mL	1 cup	**water**	
960 mL	4 cups	**milk**	**soy milk**
240 mL	1 cup	**cheddar cheese**, grated	
		or... 80 mL ⅓ cup	**nutritional yeast**
1 mL	¼ tsp	**nutmeg**	
1 mL	¼ tsp	**pepper**	
	3 slices	**bacon**, cooked crisp and cut into bits (optional)	

IMPLEMENTS

Stove • Large heavy pot • Small pot

DIRECTIONS   1:35

1 Combine the broth and barley in a large heavy pot.
Bring to a boil, reduce heat, and simmer for 45 minutes, or until the barley is tender. Stir if necessary to prevent the barley from sticking.

2 In a small pot, cook the broccoli in water until it's tender.
Drain the broccoli and add it to the barley and broth.

3 Stir in the milk *(or soy milk)*.
Heat, stirring occasionally, until hot but not boiling.

4 Stir in the cheese *(or nutritional yeast)*, nutmeg, and pepper.
Add the bacon bits if desired.

Yields 8 servings.

ⓥ 🌾 PUMPKIN SOUP

This soup can be made fresh when in season, or any time with canned pumpkin. Try adding nutmeg or cinnamon for a zestier flavor.

INGREDIENTS   *VEGAN*

30 mL	2 tbsp	**canola oil**
60 mL	¼ cup	**green bell pepper**, chopped
60 mL	¼ cup	**onion**, chopped
1 mL	¼ tsp	**pepper**
1 mL	¼ tsp	**dried thyme leaves**
	1	**bay leaf**
225 g	8 oz	**canned tomato sauce**
450 g	16 oz	**pumpkin**, mashed and cooked
480 mL	2 cups	**chicken broth** **vegetable broth**
180 mL	¾ cup	**pearl barley**
240 mL	1 cup	**half-and-half cream**
	or...	120 mL ½ cup **soy cream**
		120 mL ½ cup **soy milk**
60 mL	¼ cup	**parsley**, chopped

IMPLEMENTS

Stove • Food processor • Large heavy pot

DIRECTIONS   *1:00*

1 Heat the oil in a large, heavy pot.
Add the bell pepper and onion, then sauté for 5 minutes.

2 Add the pepper, thyme, bay leaf, tomato sauce, pumpkin, broth and barley.
Bring to a boil, reduce heat, and simmer for 25 minutes. Stir occasionally.

3 Stir in the half-and-half cream *(or soy cream and soy milk)*.
Simmering for another 5 minutes. Add salt, if desired, for taste.

4 Blend the soup in the food processor until smooth. Garnish with parsley.

Yields 8 servings.

ⓥ 🌿 ASPARAGUS SOUP

This soup is typically served hot, but in warm weather you can chill it and eat it cold.

INGREDIENTS   *VEGAN*

60 mL	¼ cup	**sliced almonds**			
30 mL	2 tbsp	**canola oil**			
	2	**leeks**, medium, white part, sliced			
	6	**scallions**, sliced			
960 mL	4 cups	**chicken broth**	**vegetable broth**		
3 mL	½ tsp	**rosemary**			
5 mL	1 tsp	**paprika**			
720 mL	2½ cups	**asparagus**, frozen or fresh, sliced			
240 mL	1 cup	**quick-cooking barley**			
240 mL	1 cup	**half-and-half cream**			
		or...	120 mL	½ cup	**soy cream**
			120 mL	½ cup	**soy milk**

IMPLEMENTS

Stove • Food processor or blender • Saucepan

DID YOU KNOW?

The cellulose in barley is located mainly in the hull and the bran. Cellulose is not digestible, so it does not provide any calories.

DIRECTIONS

1. Put the almonds and 1 tbsp (15 mL) of oil in a saucepan over medium heat.
Shake the pan while the nuts sauté, until they are a golden color.
Remove the nuts and place them on a paper towel.

2. Heat the remaining 1 tbsp (15 mL) of oil in the same pan.
Add the leeks and scallions, then cook for 5 minutes, stirring occasionally.

3. Add the broth, rosemary, paprika, asparagus, and barley to the pot.
Bring to a boil, reduce heat, and simmer for 40 minutes, or until the barley
is tender.

4. Remove the pot from the heat and let it cool slightly.

5. Puree the soup in a food processor or blender until smooth.
Blend in the half-and-half cream.

6. Return the soup to the pot and reheat it. Do not allow it to boil.
Garnish with almonds to serve.

Yields 8 servings.

ⓥ 🌾 BEEF STEW

A little heartier than soup. This makes a warming meal.

INGREDIENTS   *VEGAN*

680 g	1½ lbs	**beef stew meat**, lean			
		or...	450 g	1 lb	**seitan**
60 mL	¼ cup	**flour**			
2 mL	½ tsp	**salt**			
1 mL	¼ tsp	**pepper**			
	1	**onion**, medium, chopped			
30 mL	2 tbsp	**canola oil**			
1440 mL	6 cups	**beef broth**, low-sodium		**vegetable broth**	
240 mL	1 cup	**pearl barley**			
5 mL	1 tsp	**dried thyme**			
3 mL	½ tsp	**dried marjoram**			
1 mL	¼ tsp	**dried rosemary**, crushed			
1 mL	¼ tsp	**pepper**			
	4	**carrots**, medium, sliced			
480 mL	2 cups	**frozen cut green beans**			
30 mL	2 tbsp	**fresh parsley**, chopped			

IMPLEMENTS

Stove • Large saucepan or Dutch oven • Small bowl

DIRECTIONS

1:50

1. Combine the flour, salt, and pepper together in a small bowl.

2. Dredge the beef cubes *(or seitan)* in the flour mixture until they're coated.

3. Heat the oil in a large saucepan or Dutch oven over medium heat. Add the beef *(or seitan)* and onion, then brown them.

4. **Vegan:** Remove the seitan and set it aside.

5. Add the broth, barley, thyme, marjoram, rosemary, and pepper. Bring to a boil. Reduce heat, cover, and simmer for 1 hour.

🕐   ***... after 1 hour ...***

6. Add the carrots and green beans. Bring to a boil. Reduce heat; cover, and simmer for 20–30 minutes, or until the vegetables are tender.

7. **Vegan:** Once the mixture has gone to a simmer, add the seitan back. (Be sure to wait long enough; boiling seitan ruins its texture.)

8. Add the parsley just before serving.

Yields 8 servings.

ⓥ ❦ BEAN-AND-BUTTERNUT STEW

This a favorite among the tasters, and is nutritious, too.

INGREDIENTS

VEGAN

	1	**butternut squash**, medium		
	1	**onion**, medium, chopped		
4 cloves		**garlic**, minced		
	4	**green onions**, sliced		
2 stalks		**celery**, sliced		
45 mL	3 tbsp	**canola oil**		
225 g	8 oz	**spicy sausage**, sliced or crumbled		
	or...		225 g	8 oz **tempeh**, crumbled
			2 mL	½ tsp **salt**
			5 mL	1 tsp **garlic powder**
			2 mL	½ tsp **red chili flakes**
960 mL	4 cups	**beef broth**		**vegetable broth**
285 g	10 oz	**canned diced tomatoes**, with chilies (e.g. RO-TEL)		
5 mL	1 tsp	**black pepper**		
5 mL	1 tsp	**dried thyme**		
120 mL	½ cup	**pearl barley**		
425 g	15 oz	**canned beans**, pinto or Great Northern		
285 g	10 oz	**frozen green beans**		
120 mL	½ cup	**parsley**, chopped		
		salt (as desired for taste)		

IMPLEMENTS

Oven • Stove • Flat baking pan • Large pot

recipe continues on 114 ▶

▶ **Bean-and-Butternut Stew,** *continued from 112.*

DIRECTIONS   *1:55*

1 Preheat the oven to 400°F (205°C).
Cut the butternut squash in half and remove the seeds.
Bake the squash in a flat pan for 30 minutes, or until almost tender.

2 Remove the squash from the oven.
Peel the squash and cut it into ¾ inch (2 cm) cubes. Set the squash aside.

3 Place the onion, garlic, green onion, celery, oil, and sausage (or tempeh and seasoning) in a large pot.
Sauté for 5 minutes, or until the vegetables are soft.

4 Add the broth, tomatoes, pepper, thyme and barley to the pot.
Bring to a boil; reduce heat and simmer for 45 minutes.

🕐   *... after 45 minutes ...*

5 Add the squash and green beans.
Return to simmering and cook until the beans and barley are tender.

6 Add parsley and salt as desired for taste.

Yields 10 servings.

SUGGESTIONS
Serve with crusty bread or rolls.

CHILLED FRUIT SOUP

Our good Swedish friend, Lars Munck, gave us this traditional Scandinavian recipe. Delightful any time of year, but especially in the summer!

INGREDIENTS

1 120 mL	½ cup	**quick-cooking barley**
480 mL	2 cups	**water**
120 mL	½ cup	**dried plums**, diced
120 mL	½ cup	**dried apricots**, diced
	2	**apples**, peeled and sliced
310 g	11 oz	**canned orange segments**, with juice
450 g	16 oz	**canned cranberry sauce**
2 mL	½ tsp	**cinnamon**
1 mL	¼ tsp	**nutmeg**
60 mL	¼ cup	**sugar** (optional)

IMPLEMENTS

Stove • Heavy pot

DIRECTIONS   1:45

❶ In a heavy pot, combine the barley, water, plums, apricots, and apples. Bring to a boil, reduce heat, and simmer for 30 minutes.

❷ Add the oranges, cranberry sauce, cinnamon, nutmeg and sugar. Stir well and return to simmering until heated through.

❸ Remove the soup from the heat, cool it, and refrigerate for at least 1 hour.

❹ Once chilled, top with a dollop of sour cream or yogurt to serve.

Yields 5 servings.

MAIN COURSES

MAIN COURSES

Beef		Time	Barley
122	Garlic and Wine Tenderloin	:55	quick
125 v	Cholent	5:20	pearl
126	Sibirskie Pelmeni	1:10	flour
128 v	Mexican Beef Barley Chili	1:10	pearl
130 v	Spanish Beef Barley	1:40	pearl
132	Braised Beef with Barley	2:55	pearl
134	Sweet and Sour Unstuffed Cabbage	3:05	pearl
136 v	Zucchini Beef Pie	1:30	flakes
138 v	Sukiyaki	:55	quick
140	Meat Loaf	1:40	flakes

Lamb			
142	Lamb Shanks with Wild Rice	2:30	pearl
144	Barany Porkolt Arpakasaval	2:30	pearl

Pork			
146 v	Italian Sausage and Barley	2:00	pearl
150 v	Stuffed Peppers	1:25	pearl
152 v	Pork Chops with Barley Kraut	1:50	pearl

Calories	Balance F	P	C	Fat (g)	Prot (g)	Carb (g)	Fiber (g)	Chol (mg)
420	●	●	·	14	26	41	4 ·	60 ●
710	●	●	·	38	37	59	9 ●	140 ●
400	●	●	●	14	21	47	4 ·	155 ◉
180	●	●	·	10	14	9	2 ·	35 ●
360	●	●	·	18	21	29	6 ●	55 ●
430	●	●	·	25	36	14	3 ·	135 ●
400	·	●	●	9	20	63	10 ●	80 ●
190	·	●	·	6	20	15	2 ·	60 ●
400	●	●	·	14	19	50	5 ●	35 ·
350	●	●	·	19	26	19	3 ·	125 ◉
430	●	●	·	20	26	32	5 ●	70 ●
490	●	P	·	26	42	21	3 ·	140 ●
540	●	·	·	25	23	58	9 ●	60 ·
310	●	●	·	12	17	37	7 ●	55 ●
390	●	●	·	16	42	17	3 ·	130 ●

⚜ MAIN COURSES CONTINUED

Chicken			Time	Barley
154	v	Spicy Chicken and Pepper Stir Fry	1:25	pearl
156	v	Chicken Stew	1:05	pearl
158		Roast Chicken with Spinach Stuffing	5:15	pearl
160	v	Curry Cheese Chicken	2:00	pearl

Seafood			Time	Barley
164		Grilled Tuna	1:30	pearl
166		Baked Tilapia	1:35	pearl
168	v	Sautéed Vegetables with Shrimp	:55	pearl
170		Spicy Shrimp	1:45	pearl

Vegetable			Time	Barley
172	v	Barley Pea Pod Stir Fry	1:10	pearl
174	v	Barley Spinach Bake	1:15	pearl
176	v	Vegan Chili with Avocado Salsa	1:05	quick
178		Asparagus and Barley Frittata	1:15	pearl
180	v	Lentil Curry	1:35	pearl

Calories	Balance F	P	C	Fat (g)	Prot (g)	Carb (g)	Fiber (g)	Chol (mg)
260	·	●	·	5	24	29	5	5
320	·	●	·	8	22	42	10	50
400	●	●	·	17	36	26	6	80
570	●	·	·	25	33	52	11	100
660	●	●	·	25	56	51	12	85
320	·	●	·	10	27	31	6	55
370	●	·	·	14	15	48	9	95
480	●	·	·	17	19	56	9	115
210	●	·	·	9	8	26	6	0 -
260	·	·	●	5	7	50	10	0 -
190	·	·	●	3	7	36	9	0 -
390	●	·	·	24	21	22	5	310
360	·	·	●	10	11	59	8	5

GARLIC AND WINE TENDERLOIN

This is a delicious dish, suitable for special occasions.

INGREDIENTS

120 mL	½ cup	quick-cooking barley
120 mL	½ cup	white rice
2 mL	½ tsp	salt
480 mL	2 cups	water
	4	beef tenderloin steaks, about 4 oz each
3 mL	½ tsp	mixed herb beef seasoning
5 mL	1 tsp	olive oil
30 mL	2 tbsp	canola margarine
	4 cloves	garlic, minced
120 mL	½ cup	dry red wine
30 mL	2 tbsp	barbeque sauce

IMPLEMENTS

Stove • Medium saucepan • Large non-stick skillet

recipe continues on page 124 ▶

DID YOU KNOW?

Fatty acids are chains of two or more carbon atoms. Each carbon atom has some hydrogen atoms attached, and there's a pair of oxygen atoms at one end of the chain.

When the chain holds as many hydrogen atoms as possible, it's a *saturated* fatty acid, otherwise it's *unsaturated*. Saturated fats are solid at room temperature, while unsaturated fats are liquid (oils). Unsaturated fats are considered healthier than saturated fats.

▶ **Garlic and Wine Tenderloin,** *continued from 122.*

DIRECTIONS   :55

❶ Combine the barley, rice, salt and water in a medium saucepan.
Bring to a boil then cover, reduce heat, and simmer for 20 minutes.
Remove the barley from the heat, set aside and keep warm.

❷ Sprinkle the seasoning over the steaks and let them stand at room temperature for 15–20 minutes.

❸ Heat the olive oil and margarine in a large non-stick skillet over medium heat.

❹ Place the steaks in the skillet.
Cook for 5–7 minutes on each side for medium doneness.
Remove the steaks from the pan and keep them warm.

❺ In the same skillet, add the garlic and wine.

❻ Cook the sauce, stirring, until the browned bits in the skillet are dissolved.
Simmer another 5–10 minutes, or until the wine is reduced by half.
Stir in the barbeque sauce.

❼ Serve the steaks with the sauce and the barley rice blend on the side.

Yields 4 servings.

SUGGESTIONS
Serve with green salad and warm, crusty baguettes.
You can cook the steaks on the grill if you prefer.

ⓥ 🌾 CHOLENT

This is a traditional Jewish beef stew, not noted for being low-calorie, but favored for its cultural significance.

INGREDIENTS   *VEGAN*

	2	**onions**, sliced
30 mL	2 tbsp	**canola oil**
230 g	½ lb	**dried Lima beans**, soaked overnight in cold water
120 mL	½ cup	**pearl barley**
	3	**potatoes**, pared and quartered
680 g	1½ lbs	**brisket of beef**
	or...	480 mL 2 cups **TVP chunks**
30 mL	2 tbsp	**barley flour** (or all-purpose flour)
		salt, **pepper**, and **paprika** as desired for taste
		boiling water

IMPLEMENTS
Stove • Crock pot • Skillet

DIRECTIONS   *5:20*

❶ Brown the onions in the oil in a skillet, then place them in the crock pot.

❷ Pour in the barley, potatoes, and pre-soaked beans.
Make a space in the center and sink the meat *(or TVP chunks)* in this space.

❸ Mix the flour, salt, pepper, and paprika together. Sprinkle over the meat.

❹ Add enough boiling water to come almost to the top of the meat.

❺ Cover tightly and simmer very slowly for about 5 hours.
Do not stir, but shake the pot from time to time to prevent sticking.

Yields 6 servings.

# SIBIRSKIE PELMENI

Sibirskie Pelmeni means Siberian Dumplings. These dumplings are the Russian equivalent of Italian ravioli. Serve with melted butter or any type of meat gravy.

INGREDIENTS

240 mL	1 cup	**barley flour**
240 mL	1 cup	**all-purpose flour**
2 mL	½ tsp	**salt**
	3	**egg yolks**
120 mL	½ cup	**water**

For the filling:

340 g	¾ lb	**ground beef**
	1	**onion**, finely chopped
15 mL	1 tbsp	**water**
2 mL	½ tsp	**salt**
1 mL	¼ tsp	**pepper**
	1	**egg white**, slightly beaten

IMPLEMENTS

Stove • Large kettle • Mixing Bowl x2 • Sieve • Rolling pin and board
Slotted spoon

DID YOU KNOW?

Barley contains 2.5–3% total fat. This is similar to wheat and rye, and lower than corn (4%) or oats (7%).

DIRECTIONS

1:10 + OVERNIGHT

1. Sift the barley flour, all-purpose flour, and salt together.
   Mix in the egg yolks and enough water to make a stiff dough.

2. Knead the dough well on a lightly-floured board. Set aside for 1 hour.

🕐 *... after 1 hour ...*

3. Roll the dough out as thin as possible on a lightly floured board.
   Cut rounds or squares of pastry 3–3½ inches (8–9 cm) across.

4. In a separate bowl, create the filling by combining the beef, chopped onion, 1 tbsp (15 mL) of water, and the salt and pepper.

5. Put 1 heaping tsp (7 mL) of filling on each piece of pastry.
   Moisten the edges of the pastry with the slightly-beaten egg white.
   Fold over to form crescents or triangles and pinch the edges together.

6. If possible, chill the *pelmeni* overnight in the refrigerator.

🕐 *... the next day ...*

7. Drop the *pelmeni*, a few at a time, into a large kettle of boiling water.
   Cook at a rolling boil for 15 minutes.
   The *pelmeni* will float to the top when done.

8. Remove the *pelmeni* with a slotted spoon and drain them.

Yields 8 servings.

SUGGESTIONS

For a lunch or light supper, serve with a salad or vegetable on the side.

MEXICAN BEEF BARLEY CHILI

This chili is easy to make and tasty.

INGREDIENTS

VEGAN

450 g	1 lb	**beef stew meat**, diced small	
	or...	450 g	1 lb **diced tempeh**
	3 cloves	**garlic**, minced	
120 mL	½ cup	**onions**, chopped	
30 mL	2 tbsp	**canola oil**	
720 mL	2½ cups	**water**	
120 mL	½ cup	**pearl barley**	
410 g	14.5 oz	**canned diced tomatoes**	
225 g	8 oz	**canned tomato sauce**	
360 mL	1½ cups	**beef broth**	**vegetable broth**
240 mL	1 cup	**frozen corn**	
115 g	4 oz	**green chilies**, chopped	
15 mL	1 tbsp	**chili powder**	
3 mL	½ tsp	**ground cumin**	
		salt as desired for taste	
		pepper as desired for taste	

IMPLEMENTS

Stove • Large saucepan or Dutch oven

DIRECTIONS   *1:10*

❶ In a large saucepan or Dutch oven, cook the beef with the garlic, onion, and oil until the beef is lightly browned.
(Vegan: Do not add the tempeh yet.)

❷ Add the barley, tomatoes, tomato sauce, broth, corn, chilies, chili powder, and cumin.

❸ Bring the pot to a boil. Reduce heat, cover, and simmer for 45 minutes, stirring occasionally.
If the chili appears too thick, add extra water or broth.
Vegan: Add the tempeh after 40 minutes.

❹ Season as desired with salt and pepper.

Yields 8 servings.

SUGGESTIONS
Serve with crusty bread and grated Monterey Jack cheese.

DID YOU KNOW?
Barley is a cereal grass. The fruit of the barley plant is its seed, which is called the *grain* or *kernel*.

ⓥ 🌾 SPANISH BEEF BARLEY

This makes a great meal after a day of hiking or skiing.

INGREDIENTS   *VEGAN*

180 mL	¾ cup	**pearl barley**
360 mL	1½ cups	**water**
450 g	1 lb	**ground beef**, extra lean (15% fat)
	or... 450 g	1 lb **crumbled tempeh**
120 mL	½ cup	**onion**, chopped
120 mL	½ cup	**celery**, chopped
120 mL	½ cup	**green bell pepper**, chopped
30 mL	2 tbsp	**canola oil**
6 mL	1¼ tsp	**salt**
		pepper as desired for taste
3 mL	½ tsp	**thyme**
3 mL	½ tsp	**marjoram**
5 mL	1 tsp	**sugar**
5 mL	1 tsp	**Worcestershire sauce** vegan Worcestershire
3 mL	½ tsp	**hot pepper sauce**
410 g	14.5 oz	**canned diced tomatoes**
283 g	10 oz	**green chilies**, chopped
120 mL	½ cup	**cheddar cheese**, grated nutritional yeast
120 mL	½ cup	**black olives**, sliced (optional)
		tortilla or corn chips (optional, for garnish)

IMPLEMENTS

Oven • Stove • Saucepan • Large skillet • Casserole dish

DIRECTIONS   *1:40*

1 In a saucepan, combine the water and barley.
Bring to a boil, cover, and simmer for 40 minutes.

2 In a large skillet, sauté the ground beef (or tempeh), onion, celery and
green pepper in oil.

3 Drain off any excess fat from the beef.

4 Stir in the salt, pepper, thyme, marjoram, sugar, Worcestershire sauce, hot
pepper sauce, canned tomatoes, green chilies, and the barley.

5 Bring to a boil, then reduce heat and simmer for 10 minutes.

6 Pour the mixture into a casserole dish.
Sprinkle the grated cheese (or nutritional yeast) on top.
Lay the sliced olives on top.

7 Bake at 350°F (175°C) for 20 minutes, or until the cheese is bubbly.

Yields 6 servings.

SUGGESTIONS
If desired, form a bed of tortilla chips around the edges of the casserole.

BRAISED BEEF WITH BARLEY

This is a quick and easy meal for any season.

INGREDIENTS

1 kg	2–2½ lb	**boneless chuck roast**, trimmed of excess fat
15 mL	1 tbsp	**canola oil** or **olive oil**
	1	**onion**, medium, chopped
230 g	½ lb	**fresh mushrooms**, sliced
	3 cloves	**garlic**, minced
480 mL	2 cups	**beef broth**
	1	**bay leaf**
7 mL	1½ tsp	**salt**
1 mL	¼ tsp	**black pepper**
120 mL	½ cup	**pearl barley**
240 mL	1 cup	**frozen peas**
80 mL	⅓ cup	**sour cream** (optional)

IMPLEMENTS

Stove • Dutch oven

DID YOU KNOW?

It's not uncommon for barley to have extremely low or high levels of protein as a result of environmental effects while growing, such as available moisture or nitrogen. On average, barley contains 11–12% protein. Low-protein barley has a higher ratio of essential amino acids, while high-protein barley has more non-essential amino acids.

DIRECTIONS   *2:55*

❶ In a Dutch oven, over medium heat, brown the roast in the oil.

❷ Remove the roast and set it aside.
Drain the dutch oven, reserving 1 tbsp (15 mL) of drippings.

❸ Sauté the onions, mushrooms, and garlic in the drippings until tender.

❹ Return the roast to the pan.
Add the broth, bay leaf, salt and pepper.
Bring the pan to a boil. Reduce heat, cover, and simmer for 90 minutes.

🕒   *... after 90 minutes ...*

❺ Add the barley.
Cover and simmer for 45 minutes, or until the meat and barley are tender.

❻ Add the peas.
Cover and simmer for 5–10 minutes, or until the peas are tender.

❼ Discard the bay leaf.

❽ For a creamier gravy, mix the sour cream into the pan juices.

Yields 6 servings.

SWEET AND SOUR UNSTUFFED CABBAGE

This is an easy version of traditional stuffed cabbage, and delicious.

INGREDIENTS

	1 head	**green cabbage**
410 g	14.5 oz	**canned diced tomatoes**
230 g	8 oz	**canned tomato sauce**
120 mL	½ cup	**vinegar**
180 mL	¾ cup	**brown sugar**
30 mL	2 tbsp	**lemon juice**
360 mL	1½ cups	**water**
	1	**apple**, peeled and diced
450 g	1 lb	**ground beef**, lean
	1	**egg**
120 mL	½ cup	**pearl barley**
2 mL	½ tsp	**salt**
30 mL	2 tbsp	**raisins**

IMPLEMENTS

Stove • Large pot • Mixing bowl

DIRECTIONS   *3:05*

❶ Cut the cabbage into small chunks or shred it.

❷ Place the cabbage in a large pot with the tomatoes, tomato sauce, vinegar, brown sugar, lemon juice, water, and apple.

❸ Cover the pot, bring it to a boil, and simmer for 20–30 minutes, or until the cabbage is soft.

❹ In a mixing bowl, combine the ground beef, egg, barley, and salt.

❺ Form the beef mixture into balls and place them on top of the cabbage. Cook on low heat for 60–90 minutes.
Add the raisins and cook for another 10–15 minutes.

Yields 6 servings.

DID YOU KNOW?

More than a hundred years ago, studies found that conditions such as scurvy, rickets, beriberi, and pellagra could be prevented or cured by including a variety of foods in diets.

In 1912, Casimir Funk proposed that these helpful substances should be called "vitamines", since they were *vital* for health, and were *amines* (a type of carbon-containing molecule).

Later, it was discovered that not all "vitamines" were actually amines, so they were renamed *vitamins*.

ⓥ 🌾 ZUCCHINI BEEF PIE

A healthy, savoury meat-and-vegetable pie.

INGREDIENTS

			VEGAN
450 g	1 lb	**ground beef**, lean	**crumbled tempeh**
160 mL	⅔ cup	**barley flakes**	
160 mL	⅔ cup	**catsup**, divided in half	
120 mL	½ cup	**onion**, chopped	
	1	**egg**	**flax egg**
4 mL	¾ tsp	**salt**	
½ mL	⅛ tsp	**pepper**	
½ mL	⅛ tsp	**garlic powder**	
1 mL	¼ tsp	**hot pepper sauce**	
	2	**zucchinis**, medium, sliced	
240 mL	1 cup	**mozzarella**, shredded	**non-dairy rice mozzarella**
120 mL	½ cup	**black olives**, sliced	
3 mL	½ tsp	**oregano leaves**	
3 mL	½ tsp	**basil leaves**	
120 mL	8 tbsp	**parmesan cheese**	

	or...			
		60 mL	¼ cup	**raw cashews**
		45 mL	3 tbsp	**nutritional yeast**
		4 mL	¾ tsp	**sea salt**
		3 mL	½ tsp	**garlic powder**

IMPLEMENTS

Oven • Stove • Mixing bowl • Pie shell, 9" (23 cm) • Steaming pot

DIRECTIONS   *1:30*

1. Preheat the oven to 350°F (175°C).

2. **Vegan:** Blend the parmesan substitute ingredients in short bursts until a fairly fine, crumbly powder forms. (Do not overblend into a paste.)

3. In a mixing bowl, thoroughly mix the ground beef *(or tempeh)*, barley flakes, half of the catsup, onion, egg *(or flax egg)*, salt, pepper, garlic powder, and pepper sauce.

4. Pat the mixture into the bottom and sides of a 9" (23cm) pie shell.
Bake for 20 minutes at 350°F (175°C).

5. Remove the pie base from the oven.
Drain the moisture and fat. Set the base aside.

6. Steam the zucchini for 5 minutes. Rinse in cold water. Drain.

7. Combine half of the mozzarella cheese *(or rice mozarella)*, the remaining half of the catsup, and the black olives, oregano, and basil.

8. Spoon the mixture over the top of the meat and top it with the remaining mozzarella and the parmesan cheese *(or cashew powder)*.

9. Bake the pie for 25–30 minutes.
Remove the pie from the oven and let stand for 5 minutes.
Cut into slices.

Yields 8 servings.

SUGGESTIONS
Try substituting another vegetable in place of the zucchini.

Ⓥ 🌾 SUKIYAKI

An easy version of the traditional Japanese dish, suitable for a festive meal for company.

INGREDIENTS   *VEGAN*

120 mL	½ cup	**quick-cooking barley**	
120 mL	½ cup	**white rice**	
2 mL	½ tsp	**salt**	
480 mL	2 cups	**water**	
120 mL	½ cup	**soy sauce**, low-sodium	
30 mL	2 tbsp	**sugar**	
240 mL	1 cup	**beef broth** or stock	**vegetable broth**
60 mL	¼ cup	**mirin** (a sweet cooking rice wine)	
340 g	12 oz	**thinly-sliced beef**, such as tenderloin	
		or... 340 g 12 oz **tofu**, cubed	
60 mL	¼ cup	**sugar**	
	2	**onions**, medium, sliced	
240 mL	1 cup	**bamboo shoots**, sliced	
	2 stalks	**celery**, sliced	
240 mL	1 cup	**shiitake mushrooms**, soaked, rinsed, and sliced	
340 g	12 oz	**tofu**, cut into 1" (2.5 cm) cubes	
	1 bunch	**green onions**, cut into 2" (5 cm) lengths	
	2 leaves	**Napa cabbage**, sliced	
30 mL	2 tbsp	**vegetable oil**	

IMPLEMENTS

Stove • Electric wok (or standard wok or skillet) • Medium saucepan
Mixing bowl • Large platter

DIRECTIONS :55

1. Combine the barley, rice, salt, and water in a medium saucepan.
Bring to a boil, then cover, reduce heat, and simmer for 20 minutes.
Remove from heat, set aside, and keep warm.

2. Blend together the soy sauce, sugar, broth, and mirin in a mixing bowl.

3. Arrange the beef *(or tofu)* and the vegetables on a large platter.

4. Add oil to the electric wok or skillet and heat to 375°F (190°C).
(If using a standard wok or skillet, set burner to medium heat.)

5. Brown the beef *(or tofu)* in the oil and add the sugar slowly.
Once the beef *(or tofu)* is well-browned, move it to the corner.

6. Add the other vegetables *(and the remaining tofu)*, keeping each separate.
Add the sauce.

7. Cover, bring to a boil, and cook for 2 minutes.

8. Uncover, turn over all ingredients, and cook for 2 more minutes.

9. Serve with the barley rice blend.

Yields 4 servings.

 MEAT LOAF

Tastes good as leftover, or made into sandwiches.

INGREDIENTS

450 g	1 lb	**ground beef**, lean
450 g	1 lb	**ground pork**, lean
240 mL	1 cup	**barley flakes**
120 mL	½ cup	**onion**, chopped
60 mL	¼ cup	**green bell pepper**, chopped
60 mL	¼ cup	**celery**, chopped
5 mL	1 tsp	**salt**
3 mL	½ tsp	**pepper**
15 mL	1 tbsp	**herbs**
60 mL	¼ cup	**barbeque sauce**
10 mL	2 tsp	**Worcestershire sauce**
	2	**eggs**
120 mL	½ cup	**evaporated milk**
230 g	8 oz	**canned tomato sauce**

IMPLEMENTS

Oven • Large bowl • Baking pan, 13"x10" (33x25 cm) • Serving platter

DIRECTIONS

1:40

1. Preheat the oven to 350°F (175°C).

2. In a large bowl, mix together the beef, pork, barley flakes, onion, bell pepper, celery, salt, pepper, herbs, barbeque sauce, Worcestershire sauce, eggs and evaporated milk.

3. Form the mixture into a loaf and put it in a 13"x10" (33x25 cm) baking pan.

4. Spread the tomato sauce over top of the meat loaf.

5. Bake at 350°F (175°C) for 75 minutes.

6. Let the meat loaf stand for 5 minutes at room temperature.
   With two spatulas, loosen and transfer the meat loaf onto a serving platter. Slice and serve.

Yields 8 servings.

DID YOU KNOW?

Carbohydrates are molecules that come in various sizes, and are composed mostly of three elements: carbon (C), hydrogen (H), and oxygen (O).

Barley contains some smaller carbs, such as the "simple sugars" glucose (6 C), fructose (6 C), arabinose (5 C), and xylose (5 C).

Barley also contains huge macromolecules, such as starch and cellulose, which are formed from smaller carbs linked together.

LAMB SHANKS WITH WILD RICE

Serve with green vegetables and a salad for a hearty, healthy meal.

INGREDIENTS

450 g	1 lb	**lamb leg or shoulder**
1 mL	¼ tsp	**salt**
1 mL	¼ tsp	**pepper**
15 mL	1 tbsp	**all-purpose flour**
60 mL	¼ cup	**canola oil**, divided
240 mL	1 cup	**carrot**, diced
240 mL	1 cup	**celery**, diced
240 mL	1 cup	**yellow onion**, diced
	2 cloves	**garlic**, minced
120 mL	½ cup	**dry white wine**
430 mL	14.5 oz	**beef broth**, divided
410 g	14.5 oz	**canned diced tomatoes**, no-salt-added, incl. liquid
240 mL	1 cup	**water**
160 mL	⅔ cup	**wild rice**
80 mL	⅓ cup	**pearl barley**
5 mL	1 tsp	**dried basil**
		carrot curls (optional)
		basil sprigs (optional)

IMPLEMENTS

Oven • Stove • Large, oven-proof Dutch oven

DIRECTIONS   *2:30*

1 Trim the fat from the lamb.
   Sprinkle the lamb with salt and pepper.
   Dredge the lamb in flour.

2 Heat 2 tbsp (30 mL) of oil in a large oven-proof Dutch oven on the stove
   over medium-high heat.

3 Add the lamb. Cook for 2½ minutes on each side, or until browned.
   Remove the lamb and set it aside.

4 Add the remaining oil, plus the carrot, celery, onion, and garlic.
   Cook over medium heat for 5 minutes, or until tender.

5 Add the wine, scraping the Dutch oven to loosen the browned bits.

6 Return the lamb to the Dutch oven.
   Add 1 cup (240 mL) of the broth, plus the tomatoes, water, and dried basil.
   Cover the Dutch oven.
   Bake in the oven at 350°F (175°C) for 30 minutes.

7 Add the rice, barley, and remaining broth.
   Cover and cook for 90 minutes, until the lamb is tender and the rice done.

8 Remove the lamb from the Dutch oven.
   Remove the meat from the bone and discard the bone.

9 Shred the meat with two forks and return it to the Dutch oven.
   Garnish with carrot curls and basil sprigs, if desired.

Yields 5 servings.

BARANY PORKOLT ARPAKASAVAL

A traditional Hungarian recipe for lamb-and-barley stew.

INGREDIENTS

910 g	2 lbs	**lamb shoulder**, cut up and trimmed of excess fat
		flour (to coat the meat)
		salt as desired for taste
		pepper as desired for taste
30 mL	2 tbsp	**canola oil**
240 mL	1 cup	**onions**, chopped
	4	**tomatoes**, medium, quartered or diced
	2	**bay leaves**
60 mL	¼ cup	**pearl barley**
	6	**dried prunes**, pitted
	1 clove	**garlic**, minced
5 mL	1 tsp	**sweet paprika**
240 mL	1 cup	**water** or **broth**
30 mL	2 tbsp	**sweet cream** or **sour cream** (optional)

IMPLEMENTS

Oven • Stove • Heavy skillet or Dutch oven

DIRECTIONS

1 Using flour mixed with salt and pepper, coat the lamb pieces evenly.
In a heavy skillet or Dutch oven, brown the meat in the oil.
Brown on all sides.

2 Add the onions.
Cook until the onions are soft, but not brown.

3 Add the tomatoes, bay leaves, barley, prunes, garlic, paprika, and water.
Either... Cover and simmer over low heat for 1½–2 hours,
Or... Bake at 250°F (120°C) for 3–4 hours.

🕐 ***... after simmering or baking ...***

4 From time to time, check for moisture. If the stew is too dry, add a little
more water or broth, 1 tbsp (15 mL) at a time.
The stew should be cooked as slowly as possible.

5 Remove the stew from the heat and stir in the cream. Serve.

Yields 6 servings.

SUGGESTIONS

You can also make this recipe in a slow cooker. Set the cooker on "low"
and let it cook for 6–8 hours.

ITALIAN SAUSAGE AND BARLEY

A satisfying meal with great flavor. *(For a vegan alternative, see page 148.)*

INGREDIENTS

240 mL	1 cup	**pearl barley**
480 mL	2 cups	**water**
1 mL	¼ tsp	**salt**
450 g	1 lb	**Italian sausage** (sweet, hot, or half-and-half)
120 mL	½ cup	**onion**, chopped
	1 clove	**garlic**, minced
120 mL	½ cup	**green bell pepper**, diced
240 mL	1 cup	**fresh mushrooms**, sliced; *or...*
110 g	4 oz	**canned sliced mushrooms**, drained
240 mL	1 cup	**canned tomatoes**
120 mL	½ cup	**ketchup**
1 mL	¼ tsp	**ground basil**
1 mL	¼ tsp	**ground oregano**
2 mL	½ tsp	**sugar**
2 mL	½ tsp	**salt** (optional)
		parsley sprigs, chopped
		Romano or Parmesan cheese, grated

IMPLEMENTS

Oven • Stove • Medium saucepan • Skillet • Casserole dish

DIRECTIONS   *2:00*

❶ In a medium saucepan, combine the barley, water, and salt.
Bring it to a boil and simmer for 40 minutes.

❷ Cut the sausage into slices.
Place the slices in a skillet coated with oil and brown them lightly.
Remove the sausage from the skillet, leaving a small amount of fat.

❸ In the remaining fat, cook the onion, garlic, green pepper, and mushrooms.
Add the tomatoes, ketchup, basil, oregano, sugar, and salt.
Simmer, stirring frequently, for 5 minutes.

❹ Place the barley in a greased casserole dish.
Add the sauce and sausage.
Stir well.

❺ Bake, covered, in a preheated oven at 375°F (190°C) for 45 minutes.

❻ Top with chopped parsley and grated cheese if desired.

Yields 4 servings.

SUGGESTIONS
Serve with French bread, a crisp salad, and fresh fruit.

Ⓥ 🌾 ITALIAN TEMPEH AND BARLEY

A satisfying meal with great flavor. *(For the non-vegan recipe, see page 146.)*

INGREDIENTS

240 mL	1 cup	**pearl barley**
480 mL	2 cups	**water**
1 mL	¼ tsp	**salt**
450 g	1 lb	**tempeh**, diced
15 mL	½ tbsp	**dried basil**
15 mL	½ tbsp	**dried oregano**
3 mL	½ tsp	**onion powder**
3 mL	½ tsp	**garlic powder**
120 mL	½ cup	**onion**, chopped
	1 clove	**garlic**, minced
120 mL	½ cup	**green bell pepper**, diced
240 mL	1 cup	**fresh mushrooms**, sliced; *or...*
110 g	4 oz	**canned sliced mushrooms**, drained
240 mL	1 cup	**canned tomatoes**
120 mL	½ cup	**ketchup**
1 mL	¼ tsp	**ground basil**
1 mL	¼ tsp	**ground oregano**
2 mL	½ tsp	**sugar**
2 mL	½ tsp	**salt** (optional)
		parsley sprigs, chopped
60 mL	¼ cup	**raw cashews**
45 mL	3 tbsp	**nutritional yeast**
4 mL	¾ tsp	**sea salt**
3 mL	½ tsp	**garlic powder**

IMPLEMENTS

Oven • Stove • Medium saucepan • Skillet • Casserole dish

DIRECTIONS   *2:00*

1 Blend the raw cashews, nutritional yeast, sea salt, and garlic powder in short bursts until a fairly fine, crumbly powder forms.
Do not overblend or you will have a paste.

2 In a medium saucepan, combine the barley, water, and salt.
Bring it to a boil and simmer for 40 minutes.

3 Place the diced tempeh in a skillet coated with oil and brown it lightly.
Remove the tempeh from the skillet, leaving a small amount of oil.

4 In the remaining oil, cook the onion, garlic, green pepper, and mushrooms.
Add the tomatoes, ketchup, basil, oregano, sugar, and salt.
Simmer, stirring frequently, for 5 minutes.

5 Place the barley in a greased casserole dish.
Add the sauce and tempeh.
Stir well.

6 Bake, covered, in a preheated oven at 375°F (190°C) for 45 minutes.

7 Top with chopped parsley and cashew paste.

Yields 4 servings.

SUGGESTIONS
Serve with French bread, a crisp salad, and fresh fruit.

ⓥ 🌾 STUFFED PEPPERS

A new and colorful variation on a favourite recipe.

INGREDIENTS   *VEGAN*

240 mL	1 cup	**pearl barley**
480 mL	2 cups	**water**
	or... 960 mL 4 cups	**water**
1 mL	¼ tsp	**salt**
	4	**bell peppers**, large (any colours)
450 g	½ lb	**bulk Italian sausage**
	or... 180 mL ¾ cup	**green lentils**
240 mL	1 cup	**onion**, chopped
	2 cloves	**garlic**, minced
230 g	8 oz	**canned tomato sauce**
1 mL	¼ tsp	**dried thyme**
	vegan add: 1 mL ¼ tsp	**dried basil** *and...*
	1 mL ¼ tsp	**dried oregano**
2 mL	½ tsp	**salt**
½ mL	⅛ tsp	**pepper**

IMPLEMENTS

Oven • Stove • Medium saucepan • Large kettle • Large skillet
Baking dish, 8"x8" (20x20 cm)

DIRECTIONS

1. In a medium saucepan, combine the barley, water, and salt.
   (Vegan: also add the lentils now.)

2. Bring to a boil and simmer for 40 minutes, or until the barley is tender.
   (Vegan: lentils should also be tender.)

3. Cut the tops off the peppers and remove the seeds.

4. In a large kettle, blanch the peppers in boiling water for 3 minutes.

5. Drain the kettle, rinse the peppers in cold water, and set them aside.

6. **Non-vegan:** In a large skillet over medium heat, cook the sausage, onion, and garlic until the onion is tender and the sausage is no longer pink. Drain off the fat.

   Vegan: In a large skillet over medium heat, cook the onion and garlic until the onion is tender.

7. Stir in the tomato sauce, barley, thyme, salt, and pepper. Heat through.

8. Spoon the mixture into the peppers.
   Place the peppers in an ungreased, 8"×8" (20×20 cm) baking dish.

9. Cover and bake at 350°F (175°C) until the peppers are tender and the filling is hot.

Yields 4 servings.

ⓥ 🌾 PORK CHOPS WITH BARLEY KRAUT

This is a nice one-dish meal, and is adaptable to the slow cooker.

INGREDIENTS

Non-Vegan:

6	**pork chops**, small, trimmed of fat

Vegan:

3	**potatoes**, med., peeled and cubed in 2" (5cm) pieces
3	**carrots**, medium, peeled and cut into thick coins

INGREDIENTS, CONTINUED

			VEGAN
410 g	14.5 oz	**canned sauerkraut**	
	1	**onion**, medium, chopped	
240 mL	1 cup	**water**	
120 mL	½ cup	**pearl barley**	
30 mL	2 tbsp	**brown sugar**	
10 mL	2 tsp	**chicken bouillon** (1 cube)	**vegetable bouillon**
5 mL	1 tsp	**caraway seeds** (optional)	
1 mL	¼ tsp	**pepper**	
5 mL	1 tsp	**salt**	
120 mL	½ cup	**ketchup**	
10 mL	2 tsp	**Worcestershire**	
	or...	5 mL	1 tsp **vegan Worcestershire**

IMPLEMENTS

Oven • Mixing bowl • Baking dish, 13"x9" (33x23 cm)

DIRECTIONS
1:50

1 Mix together the sauerkraut, onion, water, barley, brown sugar, bouillon, caraway seeds, pepper, and salt.
Vegan: mix in the potatoes and carrots now as well.

2 Place the mixture in a 13"x9" (33x23 cm) baking dish.
Non-vegan: Arrange the pork chops on top of the mixture.

3 Combine the ketchup and Worcestershire.
Spread the sauce over the top of the mixture.

4 Cover the baking dish.
Bake in a preheated oven at 350°F (175°C) for 90 minutes, or until done.

Yields 6 servings.

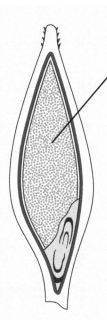

DID YOU KNOW?

The inside and largest part of the barley kernel is the *endosperm*. Inside the endosperm, there are cells where starch and proteins are stored.

The walls of these cells contain two fiber compounds, called beta-glucan and arabinoxylan, in about a 3-to-1 ratio. Along with cellulose, these two fibers make up most of the fiber in the barley kernel, regardless of whether it's covered or hull-less barley.

SPICY CHICKEN AND PEPPER STIR FRY

Quick to prepare, colorful, and tasty!

INGREDIENTS   *VEGAN*

120 mL	½ cup	**pearl barley**	
240 mL	1 cup	**water**	
½ mL	⅛ tsp	**salt**	
15 mL	1 tbsp	**canola oil**	
340 g	12 oz	**chicken tenders**	**extra-firm tofu**, cubed
	3 cloves	**garlic**, minced	
240 mL	1 cup	**scallions**, sliced	
	1	**red bell pepper**, cut into ½" (2 cm) strips	
	1	**yellow bell pepper**, cut into ½" (2 cm) strips	
60 mL	¼ cup	**soy sauce**, low-sodium	
22 mL	1½ tbsp	**rice wine vinegar**	
15 mL	1 tbsp	**fresh ginger**, minced	
10 mL	2 tsp	**Asian chili sauce**	
10 mL	2 tsp	**sesame seeds** (optional)	

IMPLEMENTS

Stove • Saucepan • Medium non-stick skillet

DIRECTIONS   *1:25*

1. In a saucepan, combine the barley, water, and salt.
   Bring to a boil and cook for 40 minutes.
   Set aside.

2. Heat the oil in a medium, non-stick skillet, over medium heat.

3. Add the chicken tenders *(or tofu cubes)*.
   Cook for 3 minutes, stirring, until browned slightly on both sides.

4 Add the garlic, scallions and bell peppers.
Cook for about 2 minutes, stirring constantly.

5 Add the soy sauce, vinegar, ginger, and chili sauce to the skillet.
Bring the mixture to a boil and cook for 1 minute.

6 Serve the mixture over the cooked barley.
Sprinkle with sesame seeds if desired.

Yields 4 servings.

ⓥ 🌾 CHICKEN STEW

A new and colorful variation on a favourite recipe.

INGREDIENTS   *VEGAN*

480 mL	2 cups	**butternut squash**, peeled and cubed
30 mL	2 tbsp	**olive oil**, divided
2 mL	½ tsp	**salt**, divided
2 mL	½ tsp	**pepper**, divided
450 g	1 lb	**chicken breasts**, boneless, skinned, diced
	or... 480 mL	2 cups **cooked chickpeas**
240 mL	1 cup	**mushrooms**, quartered
240 mL	1 cup	**onion**, chopped
240 mL	1 cup	**bell pepper** of any color, chopped
	4 cloves	**garlic**, minced
60 mL	¼ cup	**chili sauce**
430 mL	14.5 oz	**canned diced tomatoes**
	1	**zucchini**, sliced
5 mL	1 tsp	**ground cinnamon**
5 mL	1 tsp	**ground cumin**
240 mL	1 cup	**pearl barley**
15 mL	1 tbsp	**plain yogurt**, non-fat **non-dairy yogurt**
25 mL	5 tsp	**fresh cilantro**, chopped

IMPLEMENTS

Oven • Stove • Baking dish, 13"x9" (33x23 cm) • Cooking spray
Large Dutch oven

DIRECTIONS

1:05

1. Preheat the oven to 400°F (205°C).

2. Coat a 13"×9" (33x23 cm) baking dish with cooking spray.
   Combine the squash, 2 tsp (10 mL) of oil, and half of the salt and pepper.
   Toss well.
   Cover and bake for 5 minutes at 400°F (205°C).

3. Sprinkle ¼ tsp (1 mL) each of salt and pepper over the chicken.

4. Heat 2 tsp (10 mL) of oil in a large Dutch oven over medium heat.

5. Add the chicken *(or chickpeas)* and mushrooms.
   Sauté for 5 minutes, until lightly browned.

6. Remove the chicken mixture from the Dutch oven and set it aside.

7. Heat the remaining oil and add the onion, bell peppers, and garlic.
   Sauté for 3 minutes.

8. Add the chili sauce, butternut squash, chicken mixture, the remaining salt
   and pepper, and the tomatoes, zucchini, cinnamon, cumin, and barley.
   Cover, reduce heat, and simmer for 25 minutes, stirring occasionally.

9. Remove the stew from the heat.
   Stir in the yogurt.
   Ladle the stew into individual bowls and sprinkle with cilantro.

Yields 6 servings.

SUGGESTIONS

Serve with crusty bread and a salad for a complete meal.

ROAST CHICKEN WITH SPINACH STUFFING

A new twist on the original bread stuffing. The timing of this recipe is delicate, so be sure to read it through before starting.

INGREDIENTS

1.4 kg	3 lb	**whole fryer chicken**
30 mL	2 tbsp	**canola oil**
30 mL	2 tbsp	**lemon juice**
	2 cloves	**garlic**, minced
8 mL	1½ tsp	**oregano**
2 mL	½ tsp	**salt**
1 mL	¼ tsp	**pepper**
30 mL	2 tbsp	**canola oil**
120 mL	½ cup	**onion**, chopped
120 mL	½ cup	**celery**, chopped
180 mL	¾ cup	**pearl barley**
480 mL	2 cups	**chicken broth**
230 g	½ lb	**fresh spinach**, washed, stemmed, coarsely chopped
5 mL	1 tsp	**lemon peel**, grated

IMPLEMENTS

Oven • Stove • Mixing bowl • Sealable plastic bag • Saucepan
Baking pan

DIRECTIONS   5:15

❶ Wash the chicken and remove the giblets.
Place the chicken in a sealable plastic bag.

❷ Combine the lemon juice, olive oil, garlic, oregano, salt, and pepper.
Pour the mixture over chicken and seal the bag.
Marinate in the refrigerator for 2–3 hours, turning bag occasionally.

❸ Heat the oil in a saucepan over medium heat.
Add the onion, celery and barley.
Sauté until the barley is lightly browned.

❹ Stir in the chicken broth.
Cover and simmer for 45 minutes or until the liquid is absorbed.

❺ Stir in the spinach and lemon peel.
Allow the saucepan to cool.

❻ Remove the chicken from the bag, reserving any remaining marinade.
Spoon the barley stuffing into the cavity of the chicken.
Close the opening and truss.

❼ Place chicken in a baking pan.
Roast at 350°F (175°C) for 90 minutes, or until the chicken is done.
While roasing, baste occasionally with the remaining marinade.

Yields 4 servings.

CURRY CHEESE CHICKEN

This is a good way to use a leftover roast chicken. Garnish with chopped peanuts for extra appeal. *(For a vegan alternative, see page 162.)*

INGREDIENTS

240 mL	1 cup	**pearl barley**
480 mL	2 cups	**water**
30 mL	2 tbsp	**soy sauce**
30 mL	2 tbsp	**canola oil**
	3 cloves	**garlic**, minced
120 mL	½ cup	**celery**, chopped
60 mL	¼ cup	**parsley**, chopped
240 mL	1 cup	**cooked chicken**, diced
480 mL	2 cups	**green peas**
1 mL	¼ tsp	**nutmeg**
1 mL	¼ tsp	**cumin**
1 mL	¼ tsp	**turmeric**
180 mL	¾ cup	**yogurt** or **sour cream**
120 mL	½ cup	**peanuts**, chopped

Sauce:

240 mL	1 cup	**Muenster** or **Monterey Jack**, grated
40 mL	2½ tbsp	**white flour**
45 mL	3 tbsp	**cold water**
315 mL	1⅓ cups	**milk**
30 mL	2 tbsp	**butter**
2 mL	½ tsp	**salt**
10 mL	2 tsp	**curry powder**

IMPLEMENTS

Stove • Saucepan • Large skillet • Small mixing bowl

DIRECTIONS   *2:00*

1. In a saucepan, combine the barley and water.
   Bring to a boil and simmer for 40 minutes.
   Add the soy sauce to the barley and set it aside.

2. Heat the oil in a large skillet.
   Add the garlic and celery.
   Sauté over medium-low heat until the vegetables are soft

3. Add the parsley and sauté until the celery is slightly browned.

4. Add the slices of pre-cooked chicken.
   Remove from the heat and cover.

5. Using a small bowl, combine the flour and cold water.
   Mix together to form a smooth paste.

6. In a saucepan, warm the milk, butter and salt over medium-low heat.
   When just under the boiling point, whisk in the cheese a little at a time.

7. Whisk in the flour paste.
   Continue whisking until the sauce is smooth and thick.

8. Stir in the curry powder and adjust the seasonings as desired for taste.

9. Pour the curry cheese sauce over the chicken-celery mixture in the skillet.
   Add the peas, nutmeg, cumin, turmeric.
   Return to low heat until the sauce is bubbly

10. Pour the mixture over the barley.
    Add the yogurt or sour cream and mix thoroughly.
    Sprinkle peanuts over the top.

Yields 6 servings.

CHICKPEA CURRY

Garnish with chopped peanuts for extra appeal. *(For the non-vegan recipe, see page 160.)*

INGREDIENTS

240 mL	1 cup	**pearl barley**
480 mL	2 cups	**water**
30 mL	2 tbsp	**soy sauce**
30 mL	2 tbsp	**canola oil**
	3 cloves	**garlic**, minced
120 mL	½ cup	**celery**, chopped
60 mL	¼ cup	**parsley**, chopped
240 mL	1 cup	**cooked chickpeas**
480 mL	2 cups	**green peas**
1 mL	¼ tsp	**nutmeg**
1 mL	¼ tsp	**cumin**
1 mL	¼ tsp	**turmeric**
180 mL	¾ cup	**non-dairy yogurt**
120 mL	½ cup	**peanuts**, chopped

Sauce:

30 mL	2 tbsp	**olive oil**
60 mL	¼ cup	**all-purpose flour**
480 mL	2 cups	**vegetable broth**
240 mL	1 cup	**nutritional yeast**
2 mL	½ tsp	**sea salt**
1 mL	¼ tsp	**black pepper**
15 mL	1 tbsp	**Dijon mustard**
5 mL	1 tsp	**garlic powder**
10 mL	2 tsp	**curry powder**

IMPLEMENTS

Stove • Saucepan • Large skillet • Small mixing bowl

DIRECTIONS   *2:00*

❶ In a saucepan, combine the barley and water.
Bring to a boil and simmer for 40 minutes.
Add the soy sauce to the barley and set it aside.

❷ Heat the oil in a large skillet.
Add the garlic and celery.
Sauté over medium-low heat until the vegetables are soft

❸ Add the parsley and sauté until the celery is slightly browned.

❹ Add the cooked chickpeas.
Remove from the heat and cover.

❺ Heat the olive oil over medium heat in a medium saucepan.
Add the flour and whisk to form a roux.

❻ Add the vegetable broth.
Stir until no lumps remain.

❼ Add the remaining sauce ingredients.
Bring to a low boil, then reduce immediately to a simmer.
Simmer uncovered until the sauce has thickened.

❽ Pour the sauce over the chickpea-celery mixture in the skillet.
Add the peas, nutmeg, cumin, turmeric.
Return to low heat until the sauce is bubbly

❾ Pour the mixture over the barley.
Add the non-dairy yogurt and mix thoroughly.
Sprinkle peanuts over the top.

Yields 6 servings.

 GRILLED TUNA

An impressive and delicious dish for special occasions.

INGREDIENTS

80 mL	⅓ cup	**fresh lemon juice**
30 mL	2 tbsp	**extra virgin olive oil**
30 mL	2 tbsp	**fresh basil**, thinly sliced
10 mL	2 tsp	**herbs de Provence** (or your favorite herbs)
1 mL	¼ tsp	**pepper**
	3 cloves	**garlic**, minced
480 mL	2 cups	**water**
240 mL	1 cup	**pearl barley**
1 mL	¼ tsp	**salt**
480 mL	2 cups	**fresh green beans**, sliced 1" (3 cm) long
60 mL	¼ cup	**canola oil**
180 mL	¾ cup	**fennel bulb**, finely chopped
80 mL	⅓ cup	**red onion**, thinly sliced
	2	**tomatoes**, cut into wedges
30 mL	2 tbsp	**cracked pepper**
	4	**tuna steaks**, each 6 oz (170 g) and ¾" (2 cm) thick
	12	**green olives**

IMPLEMENTS

Oven or barbecue • Stove • Large saucepan • Small bowl • Whisk
Large bowl • Frying pan or skillet • Grill rack • Cooking spray

DIRECTIONS   *1:30*

❶ In a small bowl, combine the lemon juice, olive oil, basil, herbs, pepper, and garlic.
Stir well using a whisk and set aside.

❷ In a large saucepan, combine the barley, water, and salt.
Bring to a boil and simmer for 40 minutes, or until the water is absorbed and the barley is tender.

❸ Remove the barley from the heat.
Let it stand covered for about 5 minutes.
Spoon the barley into a large bowl and set aside.

❹ Drop the green beans into a large saucepan of boiling water.
Cook for 2 minutes.
Drain and rinse under cold water.
Add the beans to the barley.

❺ Using canola oil, sauté the fennel, onion, and tomatoes until tender.
Add the lemon juice. Add the vegetables to the barley mixture.

❻ Firmly press the pepper into the tuna steaks.
Place the tuna on grill rack coated with cooking spray.
Grill for 3 minutes on each side, or to desired degree of doneness.

❼ Divide the barley mixture over each tuna steak.
Add 3 olives to each serving.

Yields 4 servings.

 BAKED TILAPIA

A fish that has gained favour recently, tilapia is mild in flavor and low in fat.

INGREDIENTS

480 mL	2 cups	**water**
240 mL	1 cup	**pearl barley**
1 mL	¼ tsp	**salt**
45 mL	3 tbsp	**canola oil** or **olive oil**
120 mL	½ cup	**red onion**, chopped
10 mL	2 tsp	**garlic**, minced
240 mL	1 cup	**zucchini** or **summer squash**, chopped
240 mL	1 cup	**red or yellow bell pepper**, chopped
240 mL	1 cup	**mushrooms**, small, sliced
5 mL	1 tsp	**Worcestershire sauce**
1 mL	¼ tsp	**ground black pepper**
30 mL	2 tbsp	**balsamic vinegar**
	6	**tilapia fillets** (about 1¼ lb or 570 g)
2 mL	½ tsp	**salt**
1 mL	¼ tsp	**pepper**
1 mL	¼ tsp	**paprika**
	6	**parsley sprigs**

IMPLEMENTS

Oven • Stove • Small saucepan • Baking pan, 9"x13" (23x33 cm)
Cooking spray • Medium non-stick skillet

DIRECTIONS   *1:35*

1 Combine the water and barley in a small saucepan and bring to a boil. Reduce heat, cover, and simmer for 40 minutes, or until barley is tender. Remove from heat, uncover, and let stand.

2 Preheat the oven to 400°F (205°C). Spray a 9"x13" (23x33 cm) baking pan with cooking spray.

3 Heat the oil in a medium non-stick skillet on medium-high heat. Add the onion and garlic. Sauté 1–2 minutes.

4 Add the squash, pepper, mushrooms, Worcestershire, pepper and vinegar. Sauté until the vegetables are tender but not mushy.

5 Remove from the heat. Add the barley to the vegetables and blend well. Cover and keep the mixture warm.

6 Place the tilapia fillets in the prepared pan. Sprinkle the fish with salt, pepper and paprika. Spray with cooking spray and place in the preheated oven.

7 Bake for 15–20 minutes. (The fish is done when it flakes with a fork.)

8 Serve the fish with the barley-vegetable mixture, topped with parsley sprigs.

Yields 6 servings.

ⓥ 🌾 SAUTÉED VEGETABLES WITH SHRIMP

Barley combines well with shrimp, and this dish is quick and easy.

INGREDIENTS   *VEGAN*

15 mL	1 tbsp	**olive oil**
45 mL	3 tbsp	**canola margarine**
	1	**onion**, small, finely chopped
240 mL	1 cup	**pearl barley**
60 mL	¼ cup	**red bell pepper**, finely chopped
60 mL	¼ cup	**celery**, finely chopped
60 mL	¼ cup	**carrots**, finely chopped
120 mL	½ cup	**zucchini**, finely chopped
480 mL	2 cups	**chicken stock** or broth **vegetable broth**
230 g	8 oz	**shrimp**, medium or large, cut into ½" (2 cm) pieces
	or... 230 g 8 oz	**extra-firm tofu**, cubed
		salt as desired for taste
		pepper as desired for taste

IMPLEMENTS

Stove • Large saucepan

DID YOU KNOW?

There are two types of carbohydrates in our foods. *Soluble* carbs, which include starches and sugars, are digested and used as energy for every action of our bodies. *Insoluble* carbs don't provide energy, but are essential for the health of our digestive system. The insoluble carbs in barley include cellulose, beta-glucan (semi-soluble), and arabinoxylan, all of which are classified as dietary fiber.

DIRECTIONS :55

1. Heat the oil and 2 tbsp (30 mL) of the margarine in a large saucepan over medium heat until the margarine melts.

2. Add the onion and cook, stirring frequently, until softened (about 5 minutes).

3. Increase the heat to medium-high.
   Add the barley and cook, stirring constantly, until the barley is coated (about 1 minute).

4. Add half of the bell pepper, celery, carrots and zucchini.
   Cook, stirring frequently, for 1 minute.

5. Add the stock or broth.
   Bring the mixture to a boil.
   Cover and reduce the heat to medium-low.
   Cook, stirring occasionally, for 20 minutes.

6. Add the remaining bell pepper, celery, carrots, and zucchini.
   Add salt and pepper as desired for taste.
   Cook, uncovered, for 5 minutes.

7. Add the shrimp and cook, stirring occasionally, until the liquid has evaporated and the barley is tender (about 5–10 minutes).
   Remove the pan from the heat.

8. Stir in the remaining 1 tbsp (15 mL) of margarine until thoroughly mixed.

Yields 4 servings.

SPICY SHRIMP

This is a "wow" dish! If you're cautious with hot spice, you can leave the Tabasco out.

INGREDIENTS

240 mL	1 cup	**pearl barley**
480 mL	2 cups	**water**
1 mL	¼ tsp	**salt**
	2 strips	**bacon**, diced
	½	**green bell pepper**, chopped
	½	**onion**, large, chopped
	3 cloves	**garlic**, minced
	3	**bay leaves**
60 mL	¼ cup	**canola oil**
45 mL	3 tbsp	**flour**
1 mL	¼ tsp	**Tabasco sauce** (optional)
3 mL	½ tsp	**black pepper**, coarsely ground
2 mL	½ tsp	**salt**
3 mL	½ tsp	**celery seeds**
1 mL	¼ tsp	**thyme**
3 mL	½ tsp	**paprika**
5 mL	1 tsp	**dry mustard**
60 mL	¼ cup	**catsup**
240 mL	1 cup	**dry red wine**
340 g	¾ lb	**raw shrimp**, shelled

IMPLEMENTS

Stove • Small saucepan • Large skillet

DIRECTIONS   *1:45*

1 Combine the barley, water, and salt in a small saucepan.
Bring to a boil, reduce heat, cover, and simmer for 40 minutes, or until the barley is tender. Set aside and keep warm.

2 Sauté the bacon with the peppers, onions, garlic, bay leaves and oil in a large skillet until the vegetables are slightly soft.

3 Add the flour, Tabasco, pepper, salt, celery seed, thyme, paprika, dry mustard, catsup, and wine.
Bring to a boil. Reduce heat, cover, and simmer for 15 minutes.

4 Remove the bay leaves.
Add the shrimp and simmer for another 15 minutes.

5 Serve over the warm cooked barley.

Yields 4 servings.

BARLEY PEA POD STIR FRY

Vegetarian, tasty, and flexible. Can be served over rice. Try varying the vegetables and adding your favourites.

INGREDIENTS

120 mL	½ cup	**pearl barley**
240 mL	1 cup	**water**
170 g	6 oz	**frozen pea pods**
60 mL	¼ cup	**green onions**, sliced
240 mL	1 cup	**mushrooms**, sliced
	1 clove	**garlic**, minced
30 mL	2 tbsp	**vegetable oil**, light
30 mL	2 tbsp	**soy sauce**
115 g	4 oz	**tofu**, diced

IMPLEMENTS

Stove • Saucepan • Wok or large skillet

DIRECTIONS   *1:10*

1. In a saucepan, combine the barley and water.
Bring to a boil and simmer for 40 minutes, or until the barley is tender.
Partway through simmering, set out the pea pods to thaw.

2. In a wok or large skillet, heat the oil.
Stir-fry the pea pods, onions, mushrooms and garlic until coated with oil and crispy-tender.

3. Stir in the barley and mix well.

4. Gently fold in the tofu.
Sprinkle the soy sauce over the mixture, stirring well over the heat for about 1 minute.

Yields 4 servings.

BARLEY SPINACH BAKE

A simple and healthy vegetarian main course.

INGREDIENTS

10 mL	2 tsp	**olive oil**
	1	**onion**, large, finely chopped
	4 cloves	**garlic**, minced
240 mL	1 cup	**pearl barley**
720 mL	2½ cups	**water**
60 mL	¼ cup	**tomato paste**
5 mL	1 tsp	**chili powder**
4 mL	¾ tsp	**salt**
1480 mL	2 cups	**fresh spinach**, shredded
120 mL	½ cup	**raisins**
80 mL	⅓ cup	**almonds**, slivered and toasted

IMPLEMENTS

Oven • Stove • Non-stick Dutch oven or flameproof casserole dish

DID YOU KNOW?

The botanical name for barley is *Hordeum vulgare L.*

DIRECTIONS   *1:15*

1 Preheat the oven to 350°F (175°C).

2 In a non-stick Dutch oven or flameproof casserole dish, heat the oil on low.

3 Add the onion and garlic.
Cook, stirring frequently, until the onion is tender.

4 Stir in the barley and cook for 1 minute, stirring to coat the barley grains.

5 Add the water, tomato paste, chili powder, and salt and bring to a boil.
Cover and bake in the oven for 35 minutes.

6 Stir in the spinach and raisins.
Cover, return to the oven, and continue baking 10–15 minutes, or until the barley is tender.

7 Stir in the almonds and serve.

Yields 6 servings.

SUGGESTIONS
Try substituting another green vegetable in place of the spinach.

VEGAN CHILI WITH AVOCADO SALSA

Great as a lunch dish, with excellent flavor. The salsa can be made and used separately.

INGREDIENTS

10 mL	2 tsp	**canola oil**
240 mL	1 cup	**onion**, chopped
240 mL	1 cup	**red bell pepper**, chopped
10 mL	2 tsp	**chili powder**
5 mL	1 tsp	**ground cumin**
5 mL	1 tsp	**dried oregano**
	3 cloves	**garlic**, minced
130 g	4½ oz	**green chilies**, chopped
160 mL	⅔ cup	**quick-cooking barley**
60 mL	¼ cup	**water**
425 g	15 oz	**canned black beans**, drained
410 g	14½ oz	**canned diced tomatoes**, no-salt-added
410 g	14½ oz	**vegetable broth**
45 mL	3 tbsp	**fresh cilantro**, chopped

Avocado Salsa:

120 mL	½ cup	**avocado**, peeled and finely chopped
80 mL	⅓ cup	**tomato**, seeded and chopped
30 mL	2 tbsp	**onion**, finely chopped
15 mL	1 tbsp	**jalapeno pepper**, seeded and finely chopped
15 mL	1 tbsp	**fresh cilantro**, chopped
15 mL	1 tbsp	**fresh lime juice**
½ mL	⅛ tsp	**salt**

IMPLEMENTS

Stove • Dutch oven

DIRECTIONS   *1:05*

1 Combine the salsa ingredients and toss gently.
Yields 1 cup (240 mL) of salsa.

2 Heat the oil in a Dutch oven over medium-high heat.
Add the onion and bell pepper; sauté for 3 minutes.

3 Add the chili powder, cumin, oregano, garlic and chilies.
Cook for 1 minute.

4 Stir in the barley, water, black beans, tomatoes and vegetable broth.
Bring to a boil. Cover, reduce heat, and simmer for 20 minutes, or until barley is tender.

5 Stir in the cilantro.
Serve with sour cream, lime wedges, chips, and avocado salsa.

Yields 6 servings.

DID YOU KNOW?

The health benefits of *beta-glucans* have been recognized by scientists for some time, but most of the attention has been directed to oat products.

Barley contains just as much or more beta-glucan compared to oats. In particular, waxy barley can contain up to three times as much beta-glucan as the average oat kernel.

 ASPARAGUS AND BARLEY FRITTATA

Make this frittata a half-hour ahead and serve warm or at room temperature.

INGREDIENTS

240 mL	1 cup	**asparagus**, sliced (or 10 trimmed spears)
30 mL	2 tbsp	**olive oil**
5 mL	1 tsp	**garlic**, minced
120 mL	½ cup	**pearl barley**
240 mL	1 cup	**water**
	6	**eggs**
2 mL	½ tsp	**salt**
1 mL	¼ tsp	**pepper**
115 g	¼ lb	**Gruyere cheese**, cut into small cubes, *or...*
		cheddar cheese, grated

IMPLEMENTS

Oven • Stove • Microwave or steamer
Large, ovenproof non-stick skillet • Mixing bowl • Whisk

DID YOU KNOW?

In medieval Europe, barley was a main part of people's diets, especially poorer people. Reports from Northern Europe and Scandinavia tell of barley porridge being eaten as the main food at morning, noon and evening meals. Recent excavations in the Orkney Islands have validated these claims.

DIRECTIONS   *1:15*

1. Preheat oven broiler.

2. Microwave the asparagus in a little water until tender (or use steamer).

3. In a large, ovenproof non-stick skillet, heat the oil for 30 seconds.
   Add the garlic and cook for 1 minute.
   Add the barley and water.
   Cover and simmer for 40 minutes.

4. Add the sliced asparagus and cook for 2 minutes.

5. In a medium mixing bowl, whisk the eggs, salt, and pepper.
   Pour the mixture over the barley and asparagus.
   Cook on medium heat for 5 minutes, or until the eggs are nearly set.

6. Sprinkle with cheese.
   Broil for 1–2 minutes, just until the eggs are set and the cheese is melted.

Yields 4 servings.

SUGGESTIONS
Try substituting another vegetable in place of the asparagus.

v ⟨⟨ LENTIL CURRY

Lentils are a very good source of dietary fiber and folate, and also a source of iron, protein, zinc, potassium, and vitamins B_1 and B_6.

INGREDIENTS

			VEGAN
120 mL	½ cup	dried lentils	
120 mL	½ cup	milk	coconut milk
	1	onion, chopped	
45 mL	3 tbsp	canola margarine	coconut oil
360 mL	1½ cups	water	
5 mL	1 tsp	curry powder	
		salt as desired for taste	
		pepper as desired for taste	
120 mL	½ cup	white rice	
120 mL	½ cup	pearl barley	
480 mL	2 cups	water	
15 mL	1 tbsp	fresh lemon juice	

IMPLEMENTS

Stove • Large skillet • Saucepan • Mixing bowl

DID YOU KNOW?

Barley contains two unique carbohydrates which, although they are classified as indigestible dietary fiber, are actually partly digestible. These are *arabinoxylan* and *beta-glucan*. Beta-glucan is similar to cellulose, but with a slight difference in the links between the glucose molecules. This slight difference makes beta-glucan partly digestible.

DIRECTIONS   *1:35*

1. Wash the lentils.
   Soak them overnight in milk in the refrigerator.
   Do not drain the lentils.

2. In a large skillet, brown the onion in margarine.
   Add the lentils, milk, 1½ cups (360 mL) of water, and curry powder.
   Simmer for 1 hour, or until lentils are tender. Add more water if necessary.
   Season with salt and pepper.

3. While the lentils simmer, combine the rice, barley, and water in a saucepan.
   Cover, bring to a boil, and simmer for 40 minutes, or until the rice and
   barley are tender.

4. Add the lemon juice to the curry lentil curry.
   Serve the curry over the rice and barley mixture.

Yields 4 servings.

SUGGESTIONS
A green vegetable can be added during cooking.

pictured: Barley Stuffed Mushrooms, page 198

SIDES

 SIDES

Soups		Time	Barley
186 **v** Basic Barley Pilaf		1:15	pearl
188 **v** Mushroom and Almond Pilaf		1:10	pearl
189 **v** Barley and Beans		:45	quick
190 **v** Barley and Wild Rice Risotto		1:10	pearl
192 **v** Brown Rice, Barley, and Spinach		1:15	pearl
193 **v** Zucchini Fritters		:40	flour/cooked
194 Baked Grits and Barley with Cheese		1:05	quick
196 **v** Curried Barley and Peas		1:10	quick
197 **v** Barley and Corn Casserole		1:45	pearl
198 **v** Barley Stuffed Mushrooms		1:45	pearl
200 **v** Barley with Rice and Vegetables		1:00	quick
202 **v** Barley with Onions and Pasta		1:15	pearl
203 **v** Finnish Barley Pudding		3:10	pearl
204 **v** Toasted Barley with Vegetables		1:20	pearl

Calories	Balance F	Balance P	Balance C	Fat (g)	Prot (g)	Carb (g)	Fiber (g)	Chol (mg)	
180	●	·	●	6	4	28	6	0	-
290	●	·	·	20	6	24	7	0	-
230	●	·	·	11	5	29	7	5	•
240	●	·	·	11	7	28	5	15	•
210	·	·	●	4	5	40	4	10	•
170	●	·	·	11	4	17	3	30	●
230	●	·	·	13	10	20	3	15	•
270	●	·	●	10	7	41	10	0	-
240	·	·	●	4	6	50	8	0	-
150	●	·	·	7	3	16	3	0	-
250	·	·	●	6	8	47	8	0	-
230	·	·	●	6	6	40	7	10	•
310	●	●	●	12	11	40	6	15	•
130	·	·	●	2	5	28	7	0	-

⦿ 🌾 BASIC BARLEY PILAF

This recipe is truly a basic, provided to us long ago by Helen Eslick, wife of Bob Eslick, an inspiring barley genetics researcher.

INGREDIENTS   *VEGAN*

240 mL	1 cup	**pearl barley**	
45 mL	3 tbsp	**canola margarine**	olive oil
120 mL	½ cup	**onion**, chopped	
60 mL	¼ cup	**celery**, chopped	
60 mL	¼ cup	**green pepper**, chopped	
	1 clove	**garlic**, minced	
720 mL	2½ cups	**chicken or beef broth**	vegetable broth

IMPLEMENTS

Stove • Large saucepan

DIRECTIONS   *1:15*

1. In a large saucepan, sauté the barley, onion, celery, green pepper, and garlic in margarine until the barley is lightly browned.

2. Add the broth.
   Bring the mixture to a boil.

3. Reduce heat, cover, and simmer for 1 hour, or until the broth is absorbed.

Yields 8 servings.

MUSHROOM AND ALMOND PILAF

This is a glorified form of the Basic Barley Pilaf on page 186.

INGREDIENTS   *VEGAN*

90 mL	6 tbsp	**olive oil**
120 mL	½ cup	**slivered almonds**
240 mL	1 cup	**pearl barley**
240 mL	1 cup	**mushrooms**, chopped
120 mL	½ cup	**onion**, chopped
	4	**scallions**, with tops, sliced
120 mL	½ cup	**bell pepper**, diced
60 mL	¼ cup	**fresh parsley**, chopped
1 mL	¼ tsp	**coarse black pepper**
480 mL	2 cups	**beef broth** vegetable broth

IMPLEMENTS

Oven • Baking dish • Non-stick spray • Skillet

DIRECTIONS   *1:10*

❶ Heat the oven to 375°F (190°C).
Spray a baking dish with nonstick spray.

❷ Heat 2 tbsp (30 mL) of the oil in a skillet.
Stir-fry the almonds until lightly toasted. Remove and set aside.

❸ Add the remaining oil to the same skillet.
Sauté the barley, mushrooms, scallion and bell pepper until tender.
Remove from heat and stir in the nuts, parsley, and pepper.

❹ Place the mixture in the baking dish, pour the broth over top, and stir.

❺ Bake for 40–45 minutes.

Yields 6 servings.

BARLEY AND BEANS

Great for camping or as a quick meal.

INGREDIENTS   *VEGAN*

120 mL	½ cup	**green bell pepper**, diced	
60 mL	¼ cup	**onions**, chopped	
	3 cloves	**garlic**, minced	
60 mL	¼ cup	**canola oil**	
180 mL	¾ cup	**quick-cooking barley**	
360 mL	1½ cups	**water**	
570 g	20 oz	**canned baked beans**	pork-free baked beans

IMPLEMENTS

Stove • Skillet

DIRECTIONS   *:45*

1 Heat the oil in a skillet.
Sauté the green pepper, onion, and garlic until soft.

2 Add the barley and water.
Cover and simmer for 10–12 minutes

3 Add the baked beans.
Stir well and simmer until heated through.

Yields 8 servings.

ⓥ 🌾 BARLEY AND WILD RICE RISOTTO

A good accompaniment to beef or poultry.

INGREDIENTS   *VEGAN*

30 mL	2 tbsp	**olive oil**			
180 mL	¾ cup	**pearl barley**			
60 mL	¼ cup	**wild rice**			
120 mL	½ cup	**dry white or red wine**			
480 mL	2 cups	**beef broth** or **chicken broth**			
	or...	960 mL	4 cups	**vegetable broth**	
480 mL	2 cups	**water**		*(leave out water)*	
240 mL	1 cup	**onions**, chopped			
120 mL	½ cup	**parmesan cheese**, grated			
	or...	80 mL	⅓ cup	**raw cashews**	
		45 mL	3 tbsp	**nutritional yeast**	
		4 mL	¾ tsp	**sea salt**	
		3 mL	½ tsp	**garlic powder**	
30 mL	2 tbsp	**flat parsley**, chopped			
5 mL	1 tsp	**dried thyme**			
30 mL	2 tbsp	**unsalted butter**		**coconut oil**	

IMPLEMENTS

Stove • Large skillet

DIRECTIONS

1:10

❶ **Vegan:** Blend the parmesan substitute ingredients in short bursts until a fine, crumbly powder forms. (Do not overblend or you will have a paste.)

❷ In a large skillet, sauté the barley and wild rice in oil for 5 minutes, or until the barley is slightly browned.

❸ Add the wine.
Simmer until reduced to half.

❹ Add the broth and water *(vegan: broth only)*.
Bring to a boil.
Cover, reduce heat, and simmer for 20 minutes.

❺ Add the onions.
Cook 25–30 minutes, or until the liquid has been absorbed.

❻ Stir in the parmesan cheese *(or cashew powder)*, along with the parsley, thyme, and butter.

Yields 8 servings.

DID YOU KNOW?

An Australian research group found that people who consume barley have healthier bowel tissues. This has been attributed to *non-starch polysaccharides*, also known as *resistant starch*. Resistant starches are currently being studied for their role in controlling harmful bacteria in the bowel.

ⓥ 🌾 BROWN RICE, BARLEY, AND SPINACH

A nice combination that goes well with any main dish.

INGREDIENTS   *VEGAN*

360 mL	1½ cups	**short-grain brown rice**	
120 mL	½ cup	**pearl barley**	
480 mL	2 cups	**beef broth** or **chicken broth**	
		or...	**vegetable broth**
30 mL	2 tbsp	**canola margarine**	**coconut oil**
960 mL	4 cups	**fresh spinach**	

IMPLEMENTS

Stove • Saucepan x2 • Colander • Heat-proof serving dish

DIRECTIONS   *1:15*

❶ In a medium saucepan, combine the rice, barley, broth, and margarine *(or coconut oil)*.
Bring to a boil, cover, and reduce heat.
Simmer for 45–50 minutes.

❷ Remove the saucepan from the heat.
Let it sit, covered, for 10 minutes.

❸ Bring some water to a boil in another saucepan.
Drop the spinach in and cook for 2 minutes.
Drain the spinach into a colander.
Rinse the spinach under running cold water and chop it coarsely.

❹ Combine the rice-barley mixture and the spinach.
Place in a heat-proof serving dish and keep warm until served.

Yields 8 servings.

ⓥ 🌾 ZUCCHINI FRITTERS

These are delicious, and a great way to use zucchinis in season!

INGREDIENTS

VEGAN

480 mL	2 cups	**grated zucchini**
5 mL	1 tsp	**salt**
	1	**carrot**, grated
30 mL	2 tbsp	**onion**, minced
30 mL	2 tbsp	**parsley**, minced
	1	**egg**, beaten — flax egg
120 mL	½ cup	**barley flour**
120 mL	½ cup	**cooked barley**
	4	**basil leaves**, minced
1 mL	¼ tsp	**pepper**
		canola oil (for frying)

IMPLEMENTS

Stove • Skillet • Mixing bowl • Paper towel

DIRECTIONS

:40

❶ Mix together the zucchini and salt in a mixing bowl.
Let stand for 15 minutes.
Drain the bowl and squeeze out the liquid from the zucchini.

❷ Add the carrot, onion, parsley, egg *(or flax egg)*, flour, barley, basil, and pepper to the mixture

❸ Heat the oil in a skillet.
Drop the zucchini mixture, 1 tbsp (15 mL) at a time, into the hot oil.
Fry until golden, then drain on a paper towel before serving.

Yields 6 servings.

BAKED GRITS AND BARLEY WITH CHEESE

If you don't have regular grits, you can use quick grits and shorten the cooking time.

INGREDIENTS

	2 strips	**bacon**
60 mL	¼ cup	**onion**, chopped
600 mL	2½ cups	**water**
2 mL	½ tsp	**salt**
120 mL	½ cup	**quick barley**
120 mL	½ cup	**regular grits**
30 mL	2 tbsp	**canola margarine**
240 mL	1 cup	**cheddar cheese**, grated
60 mL	¼ cup	**parmesan cheese**, grated
1 mL	¼ tsp	**black pepper**
		paprika as desired for taste

IMPLEMENTS

Oven • Stove • Skillet • Saucepan • Baking dish, 8"x8" (20x20 cm)

DID YOU KNOW?

Barley accompanied Columbus on his trip to the Americas. However, it wasn't established as a crop at that time. Later, English settlers, including the Pilgrims in the early 1600's, established barley on the Atlantic coast. From there, it spread westward with settlers until it reached the Pacific coast.

DIRECTIONS

1:05

1. Preheat the oven to 350°F (175°C).

2. In a skillet, fry the bacon until crisp.
   Dry the bacon on a paper towel, retaining the bacon grease in the skillet.
   Remove the paper towel and cut the bacon into ½" (1 cm) pieces.

3. Sauté the onion in the bacon grease until soft.
   Add the onions to the bacon.

4. In a saucepan, combine the water, salt and barley.
   Bring to a boil. Reduce heat and simmer for 5 minutes.

5. Add the grits and cook for another 5 minutes.
   Remove the saucepan from the heat.

6. Stir the margarine, cheeses, and pepper into the barley and grits.

7. Spread the mixture in an 8"x8" (20x20 cm) baking dish.
   Sprinkle the top with paprika.

8. Bake for 30–35 minutes.

9. Top the grits with the bacon and onion mixture and serve.

Yields 6 servings.

ⓥ 🌾 CURRIED BARLEY AND PEAS

If you prefer, substitute green beans in place of the peas.

INGREDIENTS

600 mL	2½ cups	**water**
5 mL	1 tsp	**salt**
300 mL	1¼ cups	**quick-cooking barley**
60 mL	¼ cup	**canola margarine**
8 mL	1½ tsp	**curry powder**
280 g	10 oz	**frozen peas**
	1	**pimiento**, cut into strips

IMPLEMENTS

Oven • Microwave (or Stove and saucepan) • Dutch oven

DIRECTIONS   *1:10*

❶ In a Dutch oven, combine the water, salt, barley, margarine, and curry powder.

❷ Cover and bake in the oven at 400°F (205°C) for 45 minutes.

❸ Microwave the peas (or cook on the stovetop) and drain them. Gently mix the peas into the barley with a fork.

❹ Top with the pimiento strips.

Yields 6 servings.

Ⓥ 🌾 BARLEY AND CORN CASSEROLE

Great for camping or as a quick meal.

INGREDIENTS   *VEGAN*

	3 cloves	**garlic**, minced	
240 mL	1 cup	**onion**, chopped	
160 mL	⅔ cup	**carrots**, chopped	
15 mL	1 tbsp	**canola oil**	
480 mL	2 cups	**chicken broth**	vegetable broth
240 mL	1 cup	**pearl barley**	
1 mL	¼ tsp	**salt**	
½ mL	⅛ tsp	**pepper**	
480 mL	2 cups	**frozen corn**, thawed	
120 mL	½ cup	**fresh parsley**, chopped	

IMPLEMENTS

Oven • Stove • Skillet • Baking dish, 2 qt (1.8 L)

DIRECTIONS   *1:45*

❶ In a skillet over medium heat, sauté the garlic, onion and carrots in the oil until tender.

❷ Transfer the mixture to a greased 2 qt (1.8 L) baking dish.
Add the broth, barley, salt, and pepper, and mix well.

❸ Cover and bake at 350°F (175°C) for 1 hour.

🕐   *... after 1 hour ...*

❹ Stir in the corn and parsley.
Cover and bake for another 10–15 minutes, or until the barley is tender and the corn is heated through.

Yields 6 servings.

BARLEY STUFFED MUSHROOMS

These look spectacular, and taste good too!

INGREDIENTS

120 mL	½ cup	pearl barley
240 mL	1 cup	water
3 mL	¾ tsp	salt
	12	large mushrooms (or 6 portobello mushrooms)
45 mL	3 tbsp	canola oil
15 mL	1 tbsp	shallots
15 mL	1 tbsp	flour
45 mL	3 tbsp	dry sherry
½ mL	⅛ tsp	parsley
½ mL	⅛ tsp	pepper

IMPLEMENTS

Oven • Stove • Small saucepan • Skillet • Paper towel

DIRECTIONS   1:45

1. Combine the barley, water, and ½ tsp (2 mL) salt in a small saucepan. Bring to a boil, reduce heat, cover, and simmer for 40 minutes, or until the barley is tender. Set the barley aside.

2. Rinse the mushrooms and blot them dry with a paper towel. Remove the mushroom stems and finely chop them.

3. In a skillet, lightly sauté the stems and shallots in oil for 10 minutes. Add the flour, sherry, parsley, the remaining salt, and the pepper. Mix well and remove from the heat. Let cool.

4. Fill the mushroom caps with the sautéed mixture. Bake at 400°F (205°C) for 15–20 minutes.

Yields 6 servings.

BARLEY WITH RICE AND VEGETABLES

Quick, easy, and flexible.

INGREDIENTS

120 mL	½ cup	**long-grain rice**
120 mL	½ cup	**quick-cooking barley**
480 mL	2 cups	**water**
2 mL	½ tsp	**salt**
	1	**onion**, chopped
	2	**carrots**, chopped
	½	**red bell pepper**, chopped
120 mL	½ cup	**celery**, chopped
15 mL	1 tbsp	**fresh ginger**, minced
30 mL	2 tbsp	**olive oil**
280 g	10 oz	**spinach**, torn into small pieces
180 mL	¾ cup	**canned pinto beans**, drained and rinsed
15 mL	1 tbsp	**soy sauce**

IMPLEMENTS

Stove • Dutch oven • Small saucepan

DIRECTIONS   *1:00*

❶ Combine the water, salt, rice, and barley in a small saucepan.
Bring it to a boil.
Reduce heat and simmer for 12–18 minutes, or until the grains are tender.
Remove the saucepan from the heat and let it stand for 5 minutes.

❷ In a Dutch oven, sauté the onion, carrots, red pepper, celery, and ginger in oil until tender.

❸ Stir in the spinach, beans, soy sauce and rice mixture.
Cook until the mixture is heated through and the spinach is wilted.

Yields 6 servings.

SUGGESTIONS

For variety, try substituting other vegetables for the beans and spinach.

DID YOU KNOW?

Barley genetics is a science devoted to developing new barley varieties with improved traits, such as better crop yield, higher nutrition content, and other desired qualities.

All currently-available barley has been produced by standard plant breeding methods. Some recent studies have begun to investigate genetic modification techniques alongside standard breeding.

v ⁎ BARLEY WITH ONIONS AND PASTA

Easy and tasty. Add some protein and it becomes a one-dish meal.

INGREDIENTS

240 mL	1 cup	**small pasta**
30 mL	2 tbsp	**olive oil**
240 mL	1 cup	**pearl barley**
	1	**sweet onion**, sliced
230 g	½ lb	**fresh mushrooms**, sliced
480 mL	2 cups	**vegetable broth**

IMPLEMENTS

Stove • Large pot • Heavy large saucepan

DIRECTIONS   *1:15*

1. Cook the pasta until it's tender. Drain it and set it aside.

2. Heat the oil in a heavy large saucepan over medium heat.
   Add the onions and sauté for 15 minutes.

3. Add the barley and stir for 30 seconds.

4. Add the mushrooms and sauté for 5 minutes, or until the barley browns
   and the mushrooms begin to soften.

5. Add the broth and bring the mixture to a boil.
   Cover the pan. Simmer over medium-low heat for 35–40 minutes, or until
   the barley is tender and the broth is absorbed.

6. Mix the pasta into the barley.
   Season with salt and pepper as desired.

Yields 6 servings.

FINNISH BARLEY PUDDING

This is a traditional side dish. The recipe is from a wonderful Finnish gentle-man, handed down from his grandmother.

INGREDIENTS

VEGAN

360 mL	1½ cups	pearl barley	
720 mL	2½ cups	water	
1440 mL	6 cups	boiling milk	boiling soy milk
5 mL	1 tsp	salt	
2 mL	½ tsp	pepper	
80 mL	⅓ cup	butter	coconut oil
5 mL	1 tsp	canola margarine	

IMPLEMENTS

Oven • Stove • Large saucepan • Baking dish, 3 qt (2.7 L)

DIRECTIONS

OVERNIGHT + 3:10

❶ In a large saucepan, soak the barley overnight in the water.

🕐   *... the next day ...*

❷ Using the same water, cook the barley until the water is absorbed.

❸ Add the boiling milk *(or boiling soy milk)*, salt, and pepper.
Cook over low heat for 30 minutes. Stir frequently to prevent sticking.

❹ Grease a 3 qt (2.7 L) baking dish with butter *(or coconut oil)*.
Pour the barley mixture into the baking dish.
Place a dot of canola margarine on top of the mixture.

❺ Bake at 350°F (175°C) for 2 hours, or until golden brown.

Yields 8 servings.

ⓥ 🌾 TOASTED BARLEY WITH VEGETABLES

Low in calories, high in fiber, and easy to customize to your taste.

INGREDIENTS   *VEGAN*

120 mL	½ cup	**pearl barley**
415 mL	14 oz	**chicken broth** (low-sodium)
	or... 415 mL	14 oz **vegetable broth**
240 mL	1 cup	**onion**, chopped
720 mL	2½ cups	**mushrooms**, sliced
	4	**carrots**, cut in 2" (5 cm) strips
480 mL	2 cups	**cut green beans**
240 mL	1 cup	**red bell pepper**
30 mL	2 tbsp	**fresh basil**
2 mL	½ tsp	**black pepper**
	4	**scallions**, chopped

IMPLEMENTS

Stove • 12" (30 cm) skillet • Cooking spray

DID YOU KNOW?

Waxy barleys have more beta-glucans (a healthy carbohydrate), compared to non-waxy barleys. Similarly, hull-less barleys have a higher ratio of beta-glucans than covered barleys.

As a result, *waxy hull-less barley* is typically considered the most desirable type of barley for health and nutrition.

DIRECTIONS   *1:20*

1. Spray a 12" (30 cm) skillet with cooking spray.
   Cook the barley over medium heat for 6–8 minutes, stirring constantly, until golden brown.

2. Reduce the heat to low.
   Add the chicken broth *(or vegetable broth)*.
   Cover and simmer for 25 minutes, or until the barley is tender.

3. Increase the heat to high.
   Add the onion, mushrooms, carrots, green beans, bell pepper, basil, and black pepper.
   Stir until the vegetables begin to boil.

4. Reduce the heat to low.
   Cover and simmer for 20 minutes, or until the vegetables are tender.

5. Sprinkle with chopped scallions and serve.

Yields 6 servings.

SUGGESTIONS

To save time, you can use frozen mixed vegetables in place of the fresh vegetables.

BREADS

Flatbreads (cont'd)

Muffins

Scones and Biscuits

BREADS

Breads			Time	Barley
212	**v**	Sourdough French Bread	3:45	flour
214	**v**	Flake Bread	2:50	flakes
216	**v**	Sponge Bread	2:15	flour
218	**v**	Herefordshire Barley Bread	2:35	flakes
220	**v**	Austrian Peasant Bread	6:15	flour
222	**v**	Focaccia	2:35	flour
225	**v**	Finnish Barley Bread	:50	grits
226	**v**	Barley Cornbread	1:05	flour
227	**v**	Threshing Day Bread	:30	flour
228	**v**	Bagels	2:10	flour

Fruit & Vegetable Breads

230	**v**	Carrot Bread	1:45	flakes
232	**v**	Zucchini Bread	1:20	flour
234	**v**	Banana Bread	1:00	flour
236	**v**	Orange Bread	1:50	flour
238	**v**	Onion Rolls	2:35	flour

Flatbreads

240	**v**	Dill and Garlic Bread with Chilies	:50	flour
242	**v**	Swedish Flatbread	1:00	flour
244	**v**	Chapati	1:00	flour
246	**v**	Barley Maize Tortillas	:45	flour

Calories	Balance F	P	C	Fat g	Prot g	Carb g	Fiber g	Chol mg
130	-	•	◉	0	4	27	2 ●	0 -
90	•	•	●	2	2	16	1 •	0 -
90	•	•	◉	1	3	19	2 ●	0 -
140	•	•	●	3	4	27	4 ◉	0 -
80	-	•	◉	0	2	16	1 •	0 -
260	●	•	●	8	6	41	4 ●	0 -
310	●	•	●	12	6	46	8 ◉	35 ●
210	●	•	•	8	5	29	3 ●	25 ●
240	•	•	◉	2	8	48	5 ●	5 •
210	•	•	◉	2	6	44	4 ●	20 ●
220	●	•	●	10	3	31	2 •	25 ●
130	●	•	●	5	3	21	2 •	25 ●
130	●	•	●	4	2	22	2 ●	10 •
70	●	•	●	2	1	12	1 ●	10 ●
140	●	•	●	4	4	21	3 ●	0 -
80	•	•	●	2	2	14	2 ◉	0 -
200	•	•	●	3	6	38	4 ●	0 -
170	●	•	●	6	4	26	2 •	0 -
130	•	●	●	3	3	22	2 ●	0 -

✹ BREADS CONTINUED

Flatbreads (cont'd)	Time	Barley
248 **v** Malvj	2:00	flour
250 **v** Rieska	:40	flour
252 **v** Zambian Crisp Bread	1:10	flour

Muffins

	Time	Barley
254 **v** Berry Muffins	:40	flour
256 **v** Carrot and Apple Muffins	:55	flour
258 **v** Apricot Muffins	:50	flakes
260 **v** Pumpkin Muffins	:45	flakes
262 **v** Apple Bran Muffins	:45	flour
264 **v** Cranberry Walnut Muffins	:40	flakes
266 **v** Refrigerator Bran Muffins	:40	flakes
268 **v** Sesame Cheese Yeast Muffins	:50	flour

Scones and Biscuits

	Time	Barley
270 **v** Cranberry Scones	:35	flour
272 **v** Raisin Scones	:40	flour
275 **v** Apricot Scones	:40	flakes
278 **v** Fruit Mini-Scones	:35	flakes
280 **v** Bannocks	:30	flour
282 **v** Cinnamon Sweet Biscuits	:40	flour
284 **v** Angel Biscuits	:30	flour
286 **v** Barley Biscuits	:35	flour

Calories	Balance F	P	C	Fat (g)	Prot (g)	Carb (g)	Fiber (g)	Chol (mg)
130	·	·	●	1	5	26	4	0 -
190	·	·	●	5	6	33	4	5 ·
100	·	·	●	2	3	18	2	0 -
200	·	·	●	6	6	34	4	45 ●
320	●	·	·	24	5	24	3	45 ●
370	●	·	●	16	7	53	3	35 ·
250	●	·	●	10	4	38	3	15 ·
130	·	·	●	4	3	22	2	10 ·
190	·	·	●	6	4	32	2	15 ·
170	●	·	●	6	3	27	2	15 ·
140	·	●	●	3	6	22	3	15 ·
290	●	·	●	10	6	49	5	0 -
130	●	·	●	5	3	20	2	25 ●
410	●	·	●	16	8	60	2	70 ●
150	●	·	●	5	2	24	1	0 -
130	·	·	●	1	4	27	3	0 -
310	●	·	●	12	5	46	3	30 ·
220	●	·	●	9	5	32	2	0 -
80	●	●	●	3	2	12	1	0 -

SOURDOUGH FRENCH BREAD

This bread requires extra time, but has a special flavor.

INGREDIENTS

Sourdough bread:

5 mL	1 tsp	salt
600 mL	2½ cups	barley flour
600 mL	2½ cups	all-purpose flour
20 mL	4 tsp	brown sugar
12 mL	2½ tsp	active dry yeast
240 mL	1 cup	warm water
480 mL	2 cups	sourdough starter *(recipe directions below)*

Sourdough starter:

5 mL	1 tsp	active dry yeast
60 mL	¼ cup	warm water
30 mL	2 tbsp	sugar
15 mL	1 tbsp	vinegar
5 mL	1 tsp	salt
480 mL	2 cups	all-purpose flour
		warm water or warm potato water

DIRECTIONS, STARTER   :20

1. Dissolve the yeast in the warm water.
   Add the sugar, vinegar, salt, and flour. Mix well.
   Add enough potato water to make a batter—about 2 cups (480 mL).

2. Place the batter in a bowl or crock and cover loosely.
   Let stand at room temperature for 2–3 days.

   The starter is ready when it's bubbly and has a sour, yeasty odor.
   The starter can be stored covered in the refrigerator between uses.
   Add additional flour and water as needed to replenish the starter.

IMPLEMENTS

Oven • Mixing bowl x3 • Bread board • Baking sheet

DIRECTIONS, BREAD   *3:45*

❶ Mix together the salt, barley flour, and all-purpose flour.

❷ In a separate bowl, combine the brown sugar, yeast, and water to dissolve.

❸ Add the yeast mixture and the sourdough starter to the flour mixture.
Mix thoroughly and let the dough rest for 20 minutes.

❹ Knead the mixture for as long as required to achieve an elastic consistency.
Additional barley flour may be added as needed.
Place the dough in a greased bowl, cover, and let rise for 90 minutes.

🕐   *... after 90 minutes ...*

❺ On a lightly-floured bread board, knead the dough for 5 minutes.
Divide the dough in half.
Shape into two loaves.
Slice lines ½" (1 cm) deep across the loaves.

❻ Place the loaves on a greased cookie sheet.
Allow the dough to rise for an hour, or until double in size.

🕐   *... after 1 hour ...*

❼ Brush the top of the loaves with water.
Bake at 350°F (175°C) for at least 40 minutes, and until the crust is brown.

Yields 2 loaves (32 slices).

 FLAKE BREAD

This is a hearty bread with lots of fiber.

INGREDIENTS

22 mL	4½ tsp	**active dry yeast**
120 mL	½ cup	**warm water**
2 mL	½ tsp	**sugar**
530 mL	2¼ cups	**barley flakes**
60 mL	¼ cup	**molasses**
60 mL	¼ cup	**canola oil**
15 mL	1 tbsp	**salt**
240 mL	1 cup	**boiling water**
720 mL	2½ cups	**all-purpose flour**

IMPLEMENTS

Oven • Blender or food processor • Mixing bowl ×2
Large mixing bowl • Bread board • Loaf pan ×2

DIRECTIONS   *2:50*

❶ Combine the yeast, warm water, and sugar.
Let stand for 15 minutes, or until foamy.

❷ In a large bowl, combine 1 cup (240 mL) of the barley flakes with the
molasses, oil, salt, and boiling water. Cool.

❸ In a blender or food processor, grind 1 cup (240 mL) of the barley flakes
into a coarse flour.

❹ Add the coarse flour, all-purpose flour, and the yeast mixture to the
molasses mixture.
Blend to form a soft-but-not-sticky dough.
Add extra all-purpose flour if necessary.

5 Knead the dough on a floured surface for 8–10 minutes.
Add flour as needed to maintain consistency.

6 Form the dough into a ball.
Place the dough in an oiled bowl, turning the dough to grease all sides.
Cover loosely and let set in a warm place for about 30 minutes, or until doubled in bulk.

7 Punch the dough down, cut it in half, and form it into two loaves.

8 Oil two loaf pans and sprinkle the bottoms lightly with the remaining ¼ cup (60 mL) of barley flakes.
Place the loaves in the pans and cover them.
Let them rise in a warm place for an hour.

... after 1 hour ...

9 **Non-vegan:** Brush the loaves with milk.

10 Sprinkle the loaves with the remaining barley flakes.

11 Bake at 375°F (190°C) for 40–50 minutes, or until the loaves are browned and sound hollow when tapped.

Yields 2 loaves (32 slices).

v ⚜ SPONGE BREAD

The sponge process is often used for alternative flours. Yeast is allowed to bubble up with sugar and a small amount of flour. The remaining ingredients are then combined into a batter forming the bread dough.

INGREDIENTS   *VEGAN*

12mL	2½ tsp	**active dry yeast**	
410 mL	1¾ cups	**warm water**	
15 mL	1 tbsp	**brown sugar**	
11 mL	2¼ tsp	**salt**	
300 mL	1¼ cups	**warm water**	
60 mL	¼ cup	**non-fat dry milk**	soy milk powder
60 mL	¼ cup	**light molasses**	
10 mL	2 tsp	**orange peel**, grated	
480 mL	2 cups	**barley flour**	
360 mL	1½ cups	**medium rye flour**	
480 mL	2 cups	**all-purpose flour**	
15 mL	1 tbsp	**canola oil**	

IMPLEMENTS

Oven • Mixing bowl x2 • Bread pan x2

DIRECTIONS   2:15

❶ Combine the yeast, ½ cup (120 mL) of warm water, the brown sugar,
¼ tsp salt, and ½ cup (120 mL) of all-purpose flour.
Cover and let stand for 10–12 minutes, or until the yeast is slightly bubbly.

❷ Add 1¼ cups (300 mL) of warm water, the dry milk (or soy milk powder),
molasses, orange peel, the remaining salt, the barley flour, rye flour, 1 cup
(240 mL) all-purpose flour, and canola oil.

❸ Blend and work the dough for 2 minutes.
Add the remaining all-purpose flour. The dough should be soft and pliable,
but not sticky.

❹ Form the dough into a ball and cover it.
Let it set for 15 minutes.

❺ Knead the dough for 5 minutes.
Divide the dough in half and form into two balls.
Cover the dough in a greased bowl and let it stand for 25 minutes.

🕐   *... after 25 minutes ...*

❻ Shape the dough into 2 loaves and place it in greased bread pans.
Let the dough rise for 45–60 minutes.

🕐   *... after 45–60 minutes ...*

❼ Bake at 375°F (190°C) for 30 minutes, or until golden brown.

Yields 2 loaves (32 slices).

HEREFORDSHIRE BARLEY BREAD

Herefordshire is a region of northern England famous for Hereford cattle and grain farming.

INGREDIENTS

VEGAN

240 mL	1 cup	barley flakes	
240 mL	1 cup	water	
11 mL	2¼ tsp	active dry yeast (1 packet)	
60 mL	¼ cup	warm milk	warm soy milk
30 mL	2 tbsp	molasses	
2 mL	½ tsp	salt	
30 mL	2 tbsp	canola oil	
360 mL	1½ cups	barley flour	
360 mL	1½ cups	all-purpose flour	

IMPLEMENTS

Oven • Large mixing bowl x2 • Mixing bowl • Baking pan

DID YOU KNOW?

The different carbohydrates in your food are digested and absorbed at different speeds.

"Fast" carbs produce a high, steep peak in your blood sugar, which stresses your pancreas and causes your base blood sugar level to gradually increase. "Slow" carbs produce a lower, blunted, and spread-out curve.

Including more slow carbs in your diet helps to maintain a healthy level of blood sugar. Food containing fiber will also produce a "slow" carb response.

The difference between fast and slow carbs is measured by the *glycemic index* of a food. See page 367 for a comparison of glycemic index values. Barley has one of the lowest glycemic index values.

DIRECTIONS   2:35

1. Soak the barley flakes in 1 cup (240 mL) of water.
   Let stand for one hour.

🕐   *... after 1 hour ...*

2. In a large mixing bowl, blend together the yeast and milk.
   Let stand at room temperature for 10 minutes.

3. Add the soaked barley flakes, molasses, salt, and oil to the yeast mixture.
   Stir well.

4. Add the barley and all-purpose flours to the yeast mixture.
   Mix together to make a dough. If the dough is too dry, add some water.

5. Knead the dough on a floured surface until smooth.

6. Place the dough in an oiled bowl, turning to coat all sides.
   Cover the dough and put it in a warm place for 60–90 minutes, or until doubled in bulk.

🕐   *... after 60–90 minutes ...*

7. Punch down the dough, form a loaf, and place it in an oiled pan.
   Cover the dough and allow it to rise for 20 minutes.
   Meanwhile, preheat the oven to 400°F (205°C).

8. Bake the dough for 45–50 minutes.

Yields 1 loaf (16 slices).

AUSTRIAN PEASANT BREAD

The caraway seeds give this bread a European flavor.

INGREDIENTS

Sponge Riser:

11 mL	2¼ tsp	**active dry yeast** (1 packet)
80 mL	⅓ cup	**barley flour**
80 mL	⅓ cup	**all-purpose flour**
5 mL	1 tsp	**sugar**
120 mL	½ cup	**warm water**

Bread Dough:

360 mL	1½ cups	**water**
30 mL	2 tbsp	**molasses**
10 mL	2 tsp	**caraway seed**
7 mL	1½ tsp	**salt**
480 mL	2 cups	**barley flour**
480 mL	2 cups	**all-purpose flour**

IMPLEMENTS

Oven • Mixing bowl • Baking sheet

DID YOU KNOW?

Barley kernels may be the first grain ever used by humans. Remnants of barley grains and straw have been found in regions of western Asia, the Middle East and North Africa. Some remnants have been dated as far back as 10,000 years.

DIRECTIONS   *6:15*

❶ In a bowl, combine the sponge riser ingredients and blend thoroughly.
Cover and set aside in a warm place for 3 hours.

🕐   *... after 3 hours ...*

❷ Stir the sponge riser.
Add the water, molasses, caraway seed, and salt. Mix well.
Stir in the barley flour and all-purpose flour.

❸ Knead the dough for 8–10 minutes on a floured surface.
Add more flour as needed to keep from sticking.

❹ Form two round loaves and place them on a greased baking sheet.
Loosely cover the dough.
Let the dough sit in a warm place until doubled in bulk; about 2 hours.

🕐   *... after 2 hours ...*

❺ Cut four ½"-deep (1 cm deep) slashes across each loaf with a sharp knife.

❻ Bake at 375°F (190°C) for 40–45 minutes, or until the loaves are browned
and sound hollow when tapped.

Yields 2 loaves (32 slices).

 FOCACCIA

This Italian bread can be topped numerous ways to create new flavours.

INGREDIENTS   *VEGAN*

15 mL	1 tbsp	**Italian herb blend**
240 mL	1 cup	**boiling water**
11 mL	2¼ tsp	**active dry yeast** (1 packet)
5 mL	1 tsp	**sugar**
2 mL	½ tsp	**salt**
45 mL	3 tbsp	**olive oil**
300 mL	1¼ cups	**barley flour**
240 mL	1 cup	**white bread flour**
120 mL	½ cup	**Parmesan cheese**, grated

or...	120 mL	½ cup	**raw cashews**
	80 mL	⅓ cup	**nutritional yeast**
	5 mL	1 tsp	**sea salt**
	4 mL	¾ tsp	**garlic powder**

IMPLEMENTS

Oven • Large bowl • Mixing bowl • Large baking sheet

DIRECTIONS   *2:35*

❶ **Vegan:** Blend the parmesan substitute ingredients in short bursts until a fine, crumbly powder forms. (Do not overblend or you will have a paste.)

❷ In a large bowl, pour the boiling water over the herbs.
Let stand until lukewarm.

❸ Add the yeast and sugar.
Let stand 5–10 minutes or until bubbly.

recipe continues on page 224 ▶

▶ **Focaccia,** *continued from 222.*

④ Add the salt and 1 tbsp (15 mL) of olive oil.

⑤ Stir in the barley flour and bread flour.
Mix the dough until it pulls away from the bowl. (Add more bread flour to make it less sticky if needed.)

⑥ Knead the dough for 5 minutes.
Place in oiled bowl, turning to coat both sides with oil.
Cover the dough and let it sit in a warm place for 90 minutes, or until doubled in bulk.

🕐   *... after 90 minutes ...*

⑦ Punch the dough and knead for 2 minutes.

⑧ Oil a large cookie sheet.
Stretch and pat the dough into a 12"x12" (30x30 cm) square.
Cover the dough and let it rise again for 45 minutes.

🕐   *... after 45 minutes ...*

⑨ Preheat the oven to 425°F (220°C).
Using the knuckle of your forefinger, make indentations in the bread dough every 2 inches. Drizzle the oil over the top of the bread.
Vegan: Sprinkle the cashew powder over the bread.

⑩ Bake for 25 minutes, or until golden.
Non-vegan: Sprinkle the cheese over the bread.

Yields 1 loaf (6 slices).

SUGGESTIONS
Try topping the focaccia with red onion, peppers, Parmesan cheese, or sliced black olives.

FINNISH BARLEY BREAD

A truly Finnish bread! No yeast is required.

INGREDIENTS

VEGAN

480 mL	2 cups	**barley grits**	
5 mL	1 tsp	**salt**	
10 mL	2 tsp	**baking powder**	
60 mL	4 tbsp	**butter**, melted	**coconut oil**
240 mL	1 cup	**light cream**	**soy cream**
30 mL	2 tbsp	**sugar** (optional)	
120 mL	½ cup	**currants** (optional)	

IMPLEMENTS

Oven • Stove • Mixing bowl • Heavy iron skillet

DIRECTIONS

:50

1. Preheat the oven to 450°F (230°C).

2. Mix together the grits, salt and baking powder.

3. **Non-vegan:** Melt the butter in a heavy iron skillet. Add 2 tbsp (30 mL) of the melted butter to the grits mixture, leaving the rest in the skillet.
   Vegan: Add 2 tbsp (30 mL) of the coconut oil to the grits mixture.

4. Stir the cream (or soy cream) into the grits mixture.
   Add the sugar and currants (if desired).

5. Pour the batter into the skillet.
   Smooth the batter to form a layer about ½" (1.5 cm) thick.

6. Bake on the top shelf of the oven for 20–30 minutes, or until the top is lightly browned.

Yields 1 round loaf (8 slices).

Ⓥ 🌾 BARLEY CORNBREAD

This is quick and easy bread, good for any meal as a complement, and especially good with chili. Any cornmeal will work, if you can't find coarse.

INGREDIENTS   *VEGAN*

240 mL	1 cup	**coarse corn meal**	
120 mL	½ cup	**barley flour**	
120 mL	½ cup	**all-purpose flour**	
10 mL	2 tsp	**baking powder**	
2 mL	½ tsp	**salt**	
	1	**egg**	flax egg
60 mL	¼ cup	**molasses**	
60 mL	¼ cup	**canola oil**	
720 mL	2½ cups	**milk**	soy milk

IMPLEMENTS

Oven • Large mixing bowl • Small mixing bowl • Baking pan

DIRECTIONS   *1:05*

1. In a large bowl, combine the corn meal, barley flour, all-purpose flour, baking powder, and salt.

2. In a small bowl, combine the egg *(or flax egg)*, molasses, oil, and milk *(or soy milk)*.

3. Add the egg mixture to the flour mixture and mix them together.

4. Pour the combined mixture into a greased pan.

5. Bake at 350°F (175°C) for 50 minutes, or until the top is springy.

Yields 10 servings.

THRESHING DAY BREAD

This traditional bread from Northumberland, the northernmost county of England, was made with a short baking time for workers in the fields.

INGREDIENTS   *VEGAN*

830 mL	3½ cups	**barley flour**
180 mL	¾ cup	**all-purpose flour**
5 mL	1 tsp	**salt**
5 mL	1 tsp	**baking soda**
10 mL	2 tsp	**cream of tartar**
480 mL	2 cups	**buttermilk**

or...	480 mL	2 cups	**soy milk**
	10 mL	2 tsp	**apple cider vinegar**

IMPLEMENTS

Oven or griddle • Large mixing bowl

DIRECTIONS   *:30*

❶ In a large bowl, combine the barley flour, all-purpose flour, salt, baking soda, and cream of tartar.

❷ Stir in the buttermilk *(or soy milk and apple cider vinegar)* to make the dough firm.

❸ Shape the dough into a round cake, 1" (2.5 cm) thick.

❹ *Either...* Cook the cake on a very hot griddle, flipping once to cook the second side,
Or... Bake at 425°F (220°C) for 20 minutes, or until browned.

Yields 10 servings.

 BAGELS

If you've never made bagels, here's the place to start!

INGREDIENTS

			VEGAN
12 mL	2½ tsp	active dry yeast	
240 mL	1 cup	warm water	
5 mL	1 tsp	sugar	
7 mL	1½ tsp	honey	maple syrup
5 mL	1 tsp	salt	
360 mL	1½ cups	barley flour	
360 mL	1½ cups	all-purpose flour	
7 mL	1½ tsp	sugar	
2.8 L	12 cups	water	
120 mL	½ cup	bran or cornmeal	
	1	egg yolk	(leave out egg yolk)
360 mL	1½ cups	water	(leave out water)

IMPLEMENTS

Oven • Large mixing bowl • Mixing bowl • Baking sheet • Pot

DID YOU KNOW?

With the renewed interest in growing barley for food, there has been a huge movement to develop new varieties of food barley, particularly at Oregon State University and at Canadian research centers in Alberta, Manitoba and Saskatchewan. Barley foods have also been "resurrected" in many parts of Europe, especially in Scandinavia and Great Britain.

DIRECTIONS   *2:10*

1 In a large bowl, dissolve the yeast in a mixture of 1 cup (240 mL) of warm water and 1 tsp (5 mL) sugar. Let stand for 5 minutes.

2 Add the salt and honey (or maple syrup) to the yeast.

3 Slowly add the barley flour and all-purpose flour.
Knead the dough for 10 minutes.

4 Place the dough in a greased bowl and cover it.
Let the dough rise for 1 hour, or until double in bulk.

🕐   *... after 1 hour ...*

5 Knead the dough again for 7–10 minutes.
Divide the dough into 9 balls.

6 Poke your thumb through the center of each ball and work the dough into a doughnut-like shape.
Let the dough rise on a cookie sheet in a warm place.

7 Preheat the oven to 400°F (205°C).
Bring 3 qt (2.8 L) of water and 1½ tsp (7 mL) of sugar to a gentle boil.

8 Grease the cookie sheet and sprinkle it with bran.

9 Submerge the bagels into the boiling water for 5 minutes.
Lift the bagels out, drain them, and put them on the cookie sheet.

10 **Non-vegan:** Brush each bagel with a mixture of 1 egg yolk and 1½ cups (360 mL) of water.

11 Bake for 25 minutes.

Yields 9 bagels.

Ⓥ 𝄞 CARROT BREAD

This is a tasty and healthful bread, good with any meal or as a snack.

INGREDIENTS

			VEGAN
11 mL	2¼ tsp	active dry yeast (1 packet)	
60 mL	¼ cup	warm water	
5 mL	1 tsp	honey	maple syrup
120 mL	½ cup	canola oil	
120 mL	½ cup	honey	brown rice syrup
120 mL	½ cup	molasses	
	2	eggs	flax eggs
240 mL	1 cup	all-purpose flour	
180 mL	¾ cup	barley flakes	
2 mL	½ tsp	salt	
10 mL	2 tsp	cinnamon	
240 mL	1 cup	grated carrots	
120 mL	½ cup	raisins	
120 mL	½ cup	chopped nuts	

IMPLEMENTS

Oven • Large mixing bowl • Mixing bowl x2 • Loaf pan

DIRECTIONS   *1:45*

1 In a large bowl, dissolve the yeast in a combination of warm water and 1 tsp (5 mL) of honey *(or maple syrup)*.

2 Beat together the ½ cup (120 mL) of honey *(or brown rice syrup)*, oil, molasses, and eggs.
Add this mixture to the yeast mixture.

3 Combine the all-purpose flour, barley flour, salt, and cinnamon.
Add this mixture to the yeast mixture.

4 Add the carrots, raisins, and nuts. Mix together well.

5 Pour the dough into an oiled and floured loaf pan.
Place in a warm place to rise for 30 minutes.

🕐   *... after 30 minutes ...*

6 Bake at 350°F (175°C) for 1 hour.

Yields 1 loaf (16 slices).

DID YOU KNOW?

Since the start of agriculture, grains and seeds of all kinds have provided a substantial part of the nutrients we need to survive. This continues to be true today, in both developed and developing countries.

ⓥ 🌾 ZUCCHINI BREAD

This is a typical zucchini bread, but by using barley flour it becomes an extra-high-fiber bread.

INGREDIENTS   *VEGAN*

720 mL	2½ cups	**zucchini**, finely grated			
3 mL	½ tsp	**cloves**			
10 mL	2 tsp	**baking soda**			
2 mL	½ tsp	**baking powder**			
7 mL	1½ tsp	**salt**			
830 mL	3½ cups	**barley flour**			
60 mL	¼ cup	**water**			
240 mL	1 cup	**honey**			
	or...		120 mL	½ cup	**maple syrup** *and...*
			120 mL	½ cup	**brown rice syrup**
	4	**eggs**			flax eggs
160 mL	⅔ cup	**canola margarine**			coconut oil
5 mL	1 tsp	**vanilla**			

IMPLEMENTS

Oven • Mixing bowl • Large mixing bowl • Bread pan x2

DIRECTIONS

1:20

1. Preheat the oven to 350°F (175°C).

2. Grate the zucchini and set it aside.

3. Combine the cloves, baking soda, baking powder, salt, and flour. Set the mixture aside.

4. **Non-vegan:** In a large bowl, blend the water, honey, eggs, and margarine.
   Vegan: In a large bowl, blend the water, maple syrup, brown rice syrup, flax eggs, and coconut oil.

5. Add the vanilla and grated zucchini to the mixture. Fold in the flour mixture until well-blended.

6. Pour the batter into 2 greased and floured bread pans.

7. Bake for 50–60 minutes, or until a toothpick inserted in the bread comes out clean.

Yields 2 loaves (32 slices).

DID YOU KNOW?

The amount of starch in barley can vary greatly, usually due to the amount of moisture available while the plant grows. When the amount of starch in the kernel is low, the overall percentage of protein and other nutrients will be higher.

Ⓥ 🌾 BANANA BREAD

A favourite whose texture can be varied.

INGREDIENTS   *VEGAN*

360 mL	1½ cups	**all-purpose flour**
360 mL	1½ cups	**barley flour**
2 mL	½ tsp	**salt**
17 mL	3½ tsp	**baking powder**
2 mL	½ tsp	**baking spice mix**
	3	**bananas**, ripe
240 mL	1 cup	**honey**

	or...	120 mL	½ cup	**maple syrup** *and...*
		120 mL	½ cup	**brown rice syrup**

120 mL	½ cup	**canola oil**
	2	**eggs** **flax eggs**
5 mL	1 tsp	**lemon juice**
4 mL	¾ tsp	**lemon peel**, grated
180 mL	¾ cup	**walnuts**, chopped (optional)

IMPLEMENTS

Oven • Electric mixer • Mixing bowl • Bread pan x2

DIRECTIONS

1:00

1. Preheat the oven to 325°F (165°C).

2. Combine the all-purpose flour, barley flour, salt, baking powder, and baking spice mix.

3. Mash the bananas with a fork until smooth.

4. **Non-vegan:** In a mixer, blend the bananas, oil, and honey.
   Vegan: Blend the bananas, oil, maple syrup, and brown rice syrup.

5. Add the eggs (or flax eggs), lemon juice, and lemon peel.

6. Fold in the dry mixture.
   Blend at slow speed for 5 minutes.
   Fold in the walnuts (if desired).

7. Pour the dough into 2 greased and floured bread pans.
   Bake for 35–40 minutes, or until a toothpick inserted into the loaf comes out clean.

Yields 2 loaves (32 slices).

ⓥ 🌾 ORANGE BREAD

A sweeter bread that's great for breakfast or a treat.

INGREDIENTS
VEGAN

Syrup:

	2	**oranges**
120 mL	½ cup	**sugar**
120 mL	½ cup	**water**

Bread batter:

480 mL	2 cups	**barley flour**	
120 mL	½ cup	**sugar**	
2 mL	½ tsp	**salt**	
15 mL	3 tsp	**baking powder**	
	2	**eggs**, slightly beaten	**flax eggs**
45 mL	3 tbsp	**canola oil**	

IMPLEMENTS

Oven • Stove • Loaf pan x2 • Grater/zester • Saucepan
Large mixing bowl • Mixing bowl

DIRECTIONS   *1:50*

1. Oil two loaf pans and line them with waxed paper or parchment paper.

2. Grate the orange peel and squeeze out ½ cup (120 mL) of juice.

3. Combine the orange peel, ½ cup (120 mL) of sugar, and ½ cup (120 mL) of water in a saucepan.

4. Bring the syrup to a boil and simmer for 25–30 minutes.
   Let the syrup cool.

5. In a large bowl, mix together the flour, sugar, salt, and baking powder.

6. In a smaller bowl, combine the eggs (or flax eggs), syrup, oil, and the ½ cup (120 mL) of orange juice.
   Add the egg mixture to the flour mixture.

7. Pour the batter into the loaf pans.
   Bake at 350°F (175°C) for 1 hour, or until a toothpick inserted in the loaf comes out clean.

🕐   *... after 1 hour ...*

8. Cool for 10 minutes before removing from the pans.

Yields 2 loaves (32 slices).

SUGGESTIONS

For a quicker preparation, use orange juice and dried orange peel instead of fresh oranges.

ⓥ ✺ ONION ROLLS

These rolls may seem complicated to make, but are worth the effort.

INGREDIENTS   *VEGAN*

15 mL	1 tbsp	active dry yeast	
15 mL	1 tbsp	brown sugar	
300 mL	1¼ cups	warm water	
15 mL	1 tbsp	non-fat dry milk	soy milk powder
5 mL	1 tsp	salt	
120 mL	½ cup	all-purpose flour	
360 mL	1½ cups	barley flour	
240 mL	1 cup	onions, chopped	
45 mL	3 tbsp	canola margarine	coconut oil
22 mL	1½ tbsp	poppy seeds	
	1	egg white	*(leave out egg white)*
15 mL	1 tbsp	water	*(leave out water)*

IMPLEMENTS

Oven • Stove • Large mixing bowl • Mixing bowl • Small mixing bowl
Skillet • Baking sheet

DIRECTIONS   *2:35*

1 In a large bowl, dissolve the yeast and brown sugar in warm water.
Stir in the milk *(or soy milk)*, salt and all-purpose flour.

2 Add enough barley flour to form a workable dough.

3 Knead the dough on a barley-floured surface for 8–10 minutes, or until smooth.

4 Place the dough in a greased bowl.
Cover it and let it rise for 1 hour, or until double in size.

🕐   *... after 1 hour ...*

5 In a skillet, sauté the onions in margarine *(or coconut oil)* for 3–4 minutes.

6 Roll out the dough into a circle.
Spread the onions on top and sprinkle the poppy seeds over them.

7 Cut the dough into quarters, and then cut each quarter into 3 wedges.

8 Roll up each wedge, from the outside toward the center.
Place the rolls on a greased baking sheet.

9 Cover the rolls and let them rise 30–40 minutes, or until double in size.

🕐   *... after 30–40 minutes ...*

10 Preheat the oven to 350°F (175°C).

11 **Non-vegan:** In a small bowl, combine the egg white and water to make a glaze. Brush the tops of the rolls with the glaze.

12 Bake for 20 minutes, or until lightly browned.

Yields 12 rolls.

DILL AND GARLIC BREAD WITH CHILIES

A uniquely flavoured bread with an easy recipe.

INGREDIENTS   *VEGAN*

	3	**potatoes**, medium size
360 mL	1½ cups	**barley flour**
240 mL	1 cup	**all-purpose flour**
13 mL	2½ tsp	**baking powder**
60 mL	¼ cup	**fresh dill**, chopped, *or...*
7 mL	1½ tsp	**dried dill**
	3	**green chili peppers**, chopped *or...*
	1	**small can of green chili peppers**, drained
	2 cloves	**garlic**, minced
45 mL	3 tbsp	**canola oil**
4 mL	¾ tsp	**salt**
		unsalted butter (optional) *(leave out butter)*

IMPLEMENTS

Griddle • Stove • Large saucepan • Potato masher • Large mixing bowl

DIRECTIONS   :50

1 Cook the potatoes, drain them, and mash them. This should yield 2 cups (480 mL) of mashed potatoes.

2 In a large bowl, combine the mashed potatoes, barley flour, all-purpose flour, baking powder, dill, chilies, garlic, oil, and salt.

3 Mix the ingredients together with your hands until the mixture no longer sticks to sides of the bowl.

4 Divide the dough into 4 portions.
Roll each portion into a rope 6" (15 cm) long.
Cut each rope into 6 pieces, for a total of 24 pieces.

5 Roll each piece of dough into a round flatbread and dust it with flour.

6 Cook the rounds on a hot griddle, cooking on each side.
Non-vegan: If desired, brush each round with butter.

Yields 24 breads.

DID YOU KNOW?

A fat is a molecule composed of one, two, or three smaller molecules called *fatty acids*, all joined together on a molecule called *glycerol*. The compound is called a *mono-glyceride*, *di-glyceride*, or *tri-glyceride* depending on the number of fatty acids joined on the glycerol.

ⓥ 🌾 SWEDISH FLATBREAD

This bread is a classic across Scandinavia; Norway and Finland both have their own versions. This bread was my introduction into the world of barley.

INGREDIENTS

VEGAN

25 mL	5 tsp	active dry yeast	
120 mL	½ cup	lukewarm water	
480 mL	2 cups	milk	soy milk
30 mL	2 tbsp	canola margarine	coconut oil
10 mL	2 tsp	salt	
45 mL	3 tbsp	corn syrup	
3 mL	½ tsp	caraway seeds, crushed	
720 mL	2½ cups	barley flour	
480 mL	2 cups	all-purpose flour	

IMPLEMENTS

Oven • Stove • Large mixing bowl • Saucepan • Baking sheet

DID YOU KNOW?

Proteins are unique from carbohydrates and fats because they contain *nitrogen*, which is needed for building all body tissues, including muscle, skin, hair, nerves, enzymes, hormones, and blood components.

DIRECTIONS   *1:00*

❶ In a large bowl, dissolve the active dry yeast in the lukewarm water.

❷ In a saucepan, warm up the milk and margarine *(or soy milk and oil)*.

❸ Add the milk mixture to the yeast mixture.

❹ Stir in the salt, corn syrup, caraway seeds, and barley flour.

❺ Slowly fold in the all-purpose flour and work the mixture into a soft dough.
Cover the dough and let it rise for 30 minutes.

🕐   *... after 30 minutes ...*

❻ Knead the dough for 5 minutes.

❼ Divide the dough into 12 balls.
Roll out each ball to ½" (1 cm) thick.
Pierce the tops of the breads with a fork or a Swedish scored rolling pin.

❽ Bake at 500°F (260°C) on a greased cookie sheet for 6 minutes.
When cooked, the breads will have raised brown areas across the tops.
Best served warm.

Yields 12 flat breads.
Bread can be frozen and re-warmed.

CHAPATI

Barley is particularly known for its suitability for flat breads, such as this traditional Indian flat bread.

INGREDIENTS

240 mL	1 cup	**barley flour**
240 mL	1 cup	**all-purpose flour**
2 mL	½ tsp	**salt**
160 mL	⅔ cup	**water**
45 mL	3 tbsp	**canola oil**

IMPLEMENTS

Griddle • Large mixing bowl

DIRECTIONS   1:00

1. In a large bowl, combine the barley flour, all-purpose flour, and salt.

2. Slowly add the water and canola oil.
   Mix until the consistency of the dough is soft but not sticky.
   Add more flour or water as needed to achieve a soft dough.

3. Knead the dough for 8 minutes.
   Cover the dough and set it aside for 30 minutes.

🕐   *... after 30 minutes ...*

4. Divide the dough into 8 balls.
   On a floured surface, roll each ball out into a thin cake.

5. Cook on a hot griddle for less than a minute on each side.
   The breads will puff up.

Yields 8 breads.

 BARLEY MAIZE TORTILLAS

Addition of barley flour adds soluble fiber as well as important amino acids to the corn tortillas. Kari Hecker completed a nutritional research study with this recipe.

INGREDIENTS

180 mL	¾ cup	yellow corn meal
300 mL	1¼ cups	water
45 mL	3 tbsp	canola margarine
360 mL	1½ cups	barley flour
5 mL	1 tsp	salt
120 mL	½ cup	water
		extra corn meal (for rolling, if needed)

IMPLEMENTS

Griddle • Stove • Saucepan • Mixing bowl • Rolling pin • Plate

DID YOU KNOW?

Most of the barley grown in North America (30–50%) is used for feeding live-stock. The second most common use is malt barley for brewing beer. (Malting barleys are popular throughout the world of beer lovers.)

Until recently, only a small amount of North American barley was used as food, but recognition of barley's health benefits has renewed interest in eating barley.

DIRECTIONS :45

1. In a saucepan, combine the cornmeal, 1¼ cups (300 mL) of water, and the margarine.

2. Bring to a boil.
   Cover, reduce heat to low, and cook for 5 minutes.
   Turn the mixture out onto a plate and allow the cornmeal to cool.

3. Mix together the barley flour and salt.

4. Add the cooled cornmeal and ½ cup (120 mL) of water.
   Stir the mixture together and knead with your hands until smooth. (The mixture will be sticky at first, but will gradually become a smooth dough.)

5. Divide the dough into 12 balls.
   On a board dusted with corn meal, roll each ball out flat. (Turn each ball as you roll it out, to keep it round.)

6. Bake on a lightly greased hot griddle, turning to bake each side.

Yields 12 tortillas.

 MALVJ

This bread originated in Yemen. Barley bread is common in Middle Eastern countries.

INGREDIENTS   *VEGAN*

11 mL	2¼ tsp	**active dry yeast** (1 packet)
60 mL	¼ cup	**warm water**
120 mL	½ cup	**skim milk yogurt**, at room temperature
		soy yogurt, room temp.
3 mL	½ tsp	**baking soda**
240 mL	1 cup	**barley flour**
240 mL	1 cup	**whole wheat flour**
2 mL	½ tsp	**salt**

IMPLEMENTS

Griddle • Mixing bowl • Large mixing bowl

DID YOU KNOW?

Eating barley foods regularly helps to reduce heart disease, control diabetes, and improve colon health. It's believed that the majority of the health benefits of barley are due to the *beta-glucans* it contains.

DIRECTIONS   *2:00*

1. Dissolve the yeast in the warm water.

2. Stir in the yogurt *(or soy yogurt)*, then add the baking soda.

3. In a large bowl, combine the barley flour, whole wheat flour, and salt.

4. Add the yogurt mixture to the flour mixture, stirring to create a soft dough.
   Knead the dough for 10 minutes.
   Cover the dough and set it in a warm place for 90 minutes, or until
   doubled in bulk.

🕐   ***... after 90 minutes ...***

5. Knead the dough a little, then divide it into 8 balls.
   Roll each ball into a flat round.
   Cover the rounds and let them sit for 20 minutes.

6. Place the rounds on a hot, greased griddle.
   Cook for 1½ minutes, then turn and cook for 1 minute, or until done.
   During cooking, press on the dough to encourage small bubbles. (If the
   dough is not pressed, the bread will form a pocket.)

Yields 8 breads.

 RIESKA

This flatbread is quick, easy, and very good, the recipe given to me by Karen Ore.
If you've never baked with barley flour, this is a good place to start.

INGREDIENTS   *VEGAN*

480 mL	2 cups	**barley flour**			
2 mL	½ tsp	**salt**			
15 mL	1 tbsp	**sugar**			
10 mL	2 tsp	**baking powder**			
240 mL	1 cup	**evaporated milk** or **plain yogurt**			
		or...	240 mL	1 cup	**plain soy yogurt**
30 mL	2 tbsp	**canola oil**			

IMPLEMENTS

Oven • Mixing bowl • Baking sheet

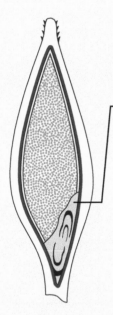

─**DID YOU KNOW?**

Beside the endosperm, protected by the hull and the bran, is the *germ* (the plant embryo). The germ is the smallest part of the kernel, and contains the genetic material to produce a new plant.

The germ is rich in high-quality protein as well as oils (lipids).

DIRECTIONS   :40

1. Preheat the oven to 450°F (230°C).

2. In a mixing bowl, mix the flour, salt, sugar, and baking powder.

3. Add the evaporated milk (or soy yogurt) and the oil.
   Stir until all the flour is moistened and a smooth stiff dough is formed.
   Add more milk (or soy yogurt) if the dough is very dry.

4. Place the dough onto a greased baking sheet.
   With the back of a spoon, form the dough into an 8" (20 cm) loaf, with a thickness of about ½" (1.5 cm).
   Prick the top of the loaf with a fork.

5. Bake for 10–15 minutes, or until the loaf is browned.

6. Cut the loaf into wedges.

Yields 1 round loaf (8 slices).

ZAMBIAN CRISP BREAD

This is another example of a flatbread that originated in an early culture.

INGREDIENTS

240 mL	1 cup	**all-purpose flour**
160 mL	⅔ cup	**barley flour**
½ mL	⅛ tsp	**salt**
5 mL	1 tsp	**sugar**
11 mL	2¼ tsp	**active dry yeast** (1 packet)
300 mL	1¼ cups	**warm water**
15 mL	1 tbsp	**canola oil**

IMPLEMENTS

Oven • Baking sheet(s) • Mixing bowl • Sieve

DID YOU KNOW?

Like all cereal grains, the major component of barley is *starch*. Starch is a large molecule composed of units of *glucose*, joined together in a way that makes the starch easy for us to digest.

DIRECTIONS

1:10

1. Oil the baking sheets and coat them thickly with flour.

2. Combine the all-purpose flour, barley flour, salt, sugar, and yeast.

3. Add the water and mix thoroughly.
   Cover and set aside for 10 minutes, or until foamy.

4. Pour the batter in a line, lengthwise along the center of the cookie sheet.
   Tilt the sheet so the batter runs across the surface.

5. Set the pan aside until the surface looks bubbly.
   Sift the extra barley flour lightly over the batter.

6. Bake at 250°F (120°C) on the top shelf of the oven for 15 minutes.

7. Score the crisp bread into pieces with a knife, and prick the top with a fork.

8. Place the pan on the middle shelf and bake for another 30 minutes.

9. Turn off the heat.
   Leave the crisp bread to cool and dry with the oven door ajar.

Yields 10 pieces.

ⓥ 🌾 BERRY MUFFINS

A low-calorie recipe with low cholesterol content.

INGREDIENTS   *VEGAN*

360 mL	1½ cups	**barley flour**	
240 mL	1 cup	**whole wheat flour**	
120 mL	½ cup	**sugar**	
5 mL	2 tsp	**baking powder**	
2 mL	½ tsp	**baking soda**	
2 mL	½ tsp	**salt**	
	2	**eggs**	**flax eggs**
300 mL	1¼ cups	**buttermilk**	

or...   300 mL   1¼ cups   **soy milk**
        6 mL   1¼ tsp   **apple cider vinegar**

60 mL	¼ cup	**unsalted butter**, melted	**coconut oil**
5 mL	1 tsp	**vanilla**	
360 mL	1½ cups	**berries** (blueberries, blackberries, or raspberries)	

IMPLEMENTS

Oven • Muffin pan • Large mixing bowl • Mixing bowl
Paper muffin-pan liners (optional)

DIRECTIONS   :40

❶ Preheat the oven to 400°F (205°C).
Grease the muffin tins or place paper liners.

❷ In a large bowl, combine the barley flour, whole wheat flour, sugar, baking powder, baking soda, and salt, mixing well.
Form a well in the center.

❸ **Non-vegan:** In a separate bowl, beat the eggs. Add the buttermilk, butter, and vanilla. Beat well.

Vegan: In a separate bowl, combine the flax eggs, soy milk, apple cider vinegar, coconut oil, and vanilla. Beat well.

❹ Pour the vanilla mixture into the well in the flour.
Mix well until blended.
Fold in the berries.

❺ Divide the batter into muffin tins.
Bake the muffins for 20–25 minutes.

Yields 12 muffins.

V ⟁ CARROT AND APPLE MUFFINS

Barley, pecans, carrots, coconut, and apple—what a flavor and nutrient combination these muffins make!

INGREDIENTS

VEGAN

240 mL	1 cup	**barley flour**	
240 mL	1 cup	**all-purpose flour**	
80 mL	⅔ cup	**brown sugar**	
10 mL	2 tsp	**baking soda**	
10 mL	2 tsp	**cinnamon**	
2 mL	½ tsp	**salt**	
	3	**eggs**	flax eggs
240 mL	1 cup	**canola oil**	
5 mL	1 tsp	**vanilla**	
120 mL	½ cup	**pecans**, chopped	
480 mL	2 cups	**grated carrots**	
120 mL	½ cup	**coconut**	
	1	**apple**, finely chopped	

IMPLEMENTS

Oven • Muffin pan • Large mixing bowl

DIRECTIONS :55

1. Preheat the oven to 350°F (175°C).
   Grease the muffin tins or place paper liners.

2. In a large bowl, combine the barley flour, all-purpose flour, sugar, baking soda, cinnamon, and salt.

3. **Non-vegan:** Beat the eggs.

4. Add the eggs *(or flax eggs)*, canola oil, and vanilla to the flour mixture.

5. Blend in the pecans, carrots, coconut, and apple until coated with batter.

6. Divide the batter into the muffin tins.
   Bake the muffins for 35 minutes, or until lightly browned.

Yields 12 muffins.

DID YOU KNOW?

About 75% of the fat in barley is made from unsaturated fatty acids, with the rest being *palmitic acid*, a saturated fatty acid. This high ratio of unsaturated fat to saturated fat is one of the positive nutritional features of barley.

ⓥ 🌾 APRICOT MUFFINS

The apricots and pecans give flavor and texture to these satisfying muffins.

INGREDIENTS   *VEGAN*

600 mL	2½ cups	all-purpose flour	
360 mL	1½ cups	barley flakes	
20 mL	4 tsp	baking powder	
5 mL	1 tsp	baking soda	
2 mL	½ tsp	salt	
2 mL	½ tsp	lemon peel	
	2	eggs	flax eggs
360 mL	1½ cups	milk	soy milk
60 mL	¼ cup	sugar	
60 mL	¼ cup	brown sugar	
120 mL	½ cup	canola oil	
5 mL	1 tsp	vanilla	
180 mL	¾ cup	dried apricots, diced	
180 mL	¾ cup	chopped pecans	

IMPLEMENTS

Oven • Muffin pan • Large mixing bowl

DIRECTIONS

:50

1. Preheat the oven to 400°F (205°C).
   Grease the muffin tins or place paper liners.

2. In a large bowl, combine the flour, barley flakes, baking powder, baking soda, salt and lemon peel.

3. Add the eggs and milk *(or flax eggs and soy milk)*, along with the sugar, brown sugar, canola oil, and vanilla.
   Mix together until well blended.

4. Stir in the apricots and pecans.

5. Divide the batter into the muffin tins.
   Bake the muffins for 25–30 minutes, or until lightly browned.

Yields 12 muffins.

DID YOU KNOW?

Obesity is increasing worldwide. There are many theories regarding the cause, from sugary drinks to fast food, but the bottom line is that people are consuming more calories than they burn up.

An important part of managing your calorie intake is satiety, which means feeling full when you've eaten enough.

Soluble fiber, such as the beta-glucans in barley, can help you to feel satiety. You should complement this with mindful eating (listening to your body) to control your food intake and manage weight.

ⓥ 🌾 PUMPKIN MUFFINS

Spicy, moist, and delicious!

INGREDIENTS

VEGAN

180 mL	¾ cup	**barley flakes**	
480 mL	2 cups	**all-purpose flour**	
120 mL	½ cup	**sugar**	
240 mL	1 cup	**brown sugar**	
15 mL	1 tbsp	**baking powder**	
5 mL	1 tsp	**pumpkin pie spice**	
2 mL	½ tsp	**baking soda**	
2 mL	½ tsp	**salt**	
2 mL	½ tsp	**cinnamon**	
240 mL	1 cup	**canned pumpkin puree**	
180 mL	¾ cup	**plain yogurt**	plain soy yogurt
	10	**prunes**, snipped into strips	
120 mL	½ cup	**canola oil**	
	1	**egg**	flax egg
30 mL	2 tbsp	**applesauce**, unsweetened	

IMPLEMENTS

Oven • Food processor • Muffin pan • Large mixing bowl • Whisk

DIRECTIONS   *:45*

1. Preheat the oven to 400°F (205°C).
   Grease the muffin tins or place paper liners.

2. In a food processor, finely grind ¼ cup (60 mL) of the barley flakes.
   Transfer the ground flakes to a large bowl.

3. Add the flour, sugar, brown sugar, and the remaining ½ cup (120 mL) of barley flakes, along with the baking powder, pumpkin pie spice, baking soda, salt, and cinnamon.
   Whisk until well-blended.

4. In a food processor, puree the pumpkin, yogurt, and prunes.

5. Add the canola oil, egg *(or flax egg)*, and the applesauce.
   Blend together.

6. Make a well in the flour mixture and pour the pumpking mixture into it.
   Stir the flour from the sides of the bowl into the pumpkin until mixed.

7. Divide the batter into the muffin tins.
   Sprinkle the tops with barley flakes if desired.
   Bake the muffins for 22 minutes, or until done.

Yields 18 muffins.

ⓥ 🌾 APPLE BRAN MUFFINS

These muffins are flavorful and healthy, with a variety of fruit and nut textures.

INGREDIENTS

VEGAN

480 mL	2 cups	**barley flour**
360 mL	1½ cups	**bran cereal**
2 mL	½ tsp	**salt**
6 mL	1¼ tsp	**baking soda**
5 mL	1 tsp	**nutmeg**
15 mL	1 tbsp	**orange peel**
240 mL	1 cup	**apple**, diced
120 mL	½ cup	**raisins**
120 mL	½ cup	**nuts**, chopped
120 mL	½ cup	**orange juice**
480 mL	2 cups	**buttermilk**

		or...	480 mL	2 cups	**soy milk**
			10 mL	2 tsp	**apple cider vinegar**

	1	**egg**

flax egg

30 mL	2 tbsp	**molasses**
80 mL	⅓ cup	**sugar**
30 mL	2 tbsp	**canola oil**

IMPLEMENTS

Oven • Muffin pan • Mixing bowl • Grater/zester • Small mixing bowl

DIRECTIONS   :45

1. Preheat the oven to 350°F (175°C).
   Grease the muffin tins or place paper liners.

2. Combine the flour, bran, salt, baking soda, and nutmeg.

3. Stir in the orange peel, apples, raisins and nuts.

4. Add the orange juice and buttermilk *(or soy milk and apple cider vinegar)*.

5. In a small bowl, beat the egg *(or flax egg)* together with the molasses, sugar, and canola oil.
   Add the molasses mixture to the batter.

6. Divide the batter into the muffin tins.
   Bake the muffins for 25 minutes, or until lightly browned.

Yields 18 muffins.

DID YOU KNOW?

Neither barley, nor any other food, can prevent diabetes or control carbohydrate metabolism on its own. For a complete approach, we recommend the *Glucose Revolution Plan*, developed by Dr. Jennie Brand Miller, an Australian author and nutrition researcher. (See Bibliography on page 370.)

CRANBERRY WALNUT MUFFINS

Good flavor and texture in these easy-to-make muffins.

INGREDIENTS   *VEGAN*

240 mL	1 cup	**all-purpose flour**
240 mL	1 cup	**barley flakes**
80 mL	1/3 cup	**brown sugar**
12 mL	2½ tsp	**baking powder**
2 mL	½ tsp	**salt**
2 mL	½ tsp	**cinnamon**
120 mL	½ cup	**dried cranberries**
120 mL	½ cup	**walnuts**, chopped
240 mL	1 cup	**vanilla yogurt**

or... 240 mL 1 cup **plain soy yogurt**
        5 mL 1 tsp **vanilla**
       10 mL 2 tsp **maple syrup**

	1	**egg**	**flax egg**
30 mL	2 tbsp	**canola oil**

IMPLEMENTS

Oven • Muffin pan • Large mixing bowl • Small mixing bowl • Whisk

DIRECTIONS   *:40*

1 Preheat the oven to 400°F (205°C).
Lightly grease the muffin tins or place paper liners.

2 In a large bowl, combine the all-purpose flour, barley flakes, brown sugar, baking powder, salt, and cinnamon.

3 Stir in the cranberries and walnuts.

4 **Non-vegan:** In a small bowl, whisk together the yogurt, egg, and oil.

Vegan: In a small bowl, whisk together the soy yogurt, vanilla, maple syrup, flax egg, and oil.

5 Stir the yogurt mixture into the flour mixture, just enough to create a moist batter.

6 Divide the batter into 12 muffin tins.
Bake the muffins for 20–25 minutes.

Yields 12 muffins.

ⓥ ⫷ REFRIGERATOR BRAN MUFFINS

Have muffins whenever you want by making up a large container of batter and storing it in the refrigerator. You can bake as few or as many as you want each time.

INGREDIENTS

VEGAN

480 mL	2 cups	boiling water				
1440 mL	6 cups	bran flakes				
240 mL	1 cup	canola oil				
240 mL	1 cup	sugar				
240 mL	1 cup	brown sugar				
240 mL	1 cup	molasses				
	4	eggs				flax eggs
960 mL	4 cups	buttermilk				
		or...	960 mL	4 cups	soy milk	
			20 mL	4 tsp	apple cider vinegar	
1200 mL	5 cups	barley flour				
25 mL	5 tsp	baking soda				
10 mL	2 tsp	salt				

IMPLEMENTS

Oven • Muffin pan • Large mixing bowl • Mixing bowl

DIRECTIONS   :40

1. Preheat the oven to 400°F (205°C).
   Grease the muffin tins or place paper liners.

2. Pour boiling water over 2 cups (480 mL) of the bran flakes.
   Set aside to cool slightly.

3. In a large bowl, combine the oil, sugar, brown sugar, and molasses.

4. **Non-vegan:** Add the eggs and buttermilk to the large bowl and mix together.

   Vegan: Add the flax eggs, soy milk, and apple cider vinegar to the large bowl and mix together.

5. In another bowl, mix together the flour, baking soda, and salt.
   Add the flour mixture to the large bowl.
   Add the soaked bran flakes and remaining bran flakes to the large bowl.
   Stir everything to form a batter.

6. Divide the batter into the muffin tins.
   Store unused batter in the refrigerator.
   Bake the muffins for 18 minutes, or until lightly browned.

Yields 48 muffins.
Batter can be stored in the refrigerator for up to 4 weeks.

ⓥ 🌾 SESAME CHEESE YEAST MUFFINS

These muffins are high in protein and delicious. They require extra time for the yeast development.

INGREDIENTS   *VEGAN*

30 mL	2 tbsp	**onion**, minced			
15 mL	1 tbsp	**canola oil**			
240 mL	1 cup	**cottage cheese**			
	or...		240 mL	1 cup	**firm tofu**
			80 mL	⅓ cup	**vegan mayonnaise**
			2 mL	½ tsp	**garlic powder**
			2 mL	½ tsp	**onion powder**
			2 mL	½ tsp	**sea salt**
30 mL	2 tbsp	**brown sugar**			
5 mL	1 tsp	**salt**			
15 mL	1 tbsp	**sesame seeds**			
11 mL	2¼ tsp	**active dry yeast** (1 packet)			
80 mL	⅓ cup	**warm water**			
	1	**egg**		*flax egg*	
300 mL	1¼ cups	**barley flour**			
240 mL	1 cup	**whole wheat flour**			

IMPLEMENTS

Oven • Stove • Muffin pan • Skillet • Large mixing bowl • Bread board

DIRECTIONS :50

1 **Vegan:** Blend the cottage cheese substitute ingredients to achieve a consistency like cottage cheese (blended but a bit chunky).

2 Preheat the oven to 400°F (205°C).
Grease the muffin tins or place paper liners.

3 Sauté the minced onion in the oil until soft.
Add the cottage cheese *(or tofu mix)*, brown sugar, salt, and sesame seeds.

4 In a large bowl, dissolve the yeast in warm water.
Add the warm onion mixture, egg *(or flax egg)* and barley flour and mix.
Add the whole wheat flour.
Mix to form a dough.

5 On a lightly-floured board, turn out the dough.
Knead the dough until smooth.

6 Divide the dough into 12 balls and place in the muffin pan.

7 Cover the pan lightly with plastic wrap and put it in a warm place.
Allow the dough to rise until double in size.

8 Bake the muffins 15–18 minutes, or until lightly browned.

Yields 12 muffins.

ⓥ 🌾 CRANBERRY SCONES

Tart cranberries and sweet cinnamon sugar combine to create these delightful scones.

INGREDIENTS

VEGAN

240 mL	1 cup	all-purpose flour	
120 mL	½ cup	barley flour	
2 mL	½ tsp	salt	
5 mL	1 tsp	baking soda	
240 mL	1 cup	barley flakes	
60 mL	¼ cup	brown sugar	
60 mL	¼ cup	canola margarine	coconut oil
120 mL	½ cup	dried cranberries	
240 mL	1 cup	mashed banana	
15 mL	1 tbsp	lemon juice	
120 mL	½ cup	sliced almonds	
		cinnamon sugar (optional)	

IMPLEMENTS

Oven • Large mixing bowl • Bread board • Baking sheet

DID YOU KNOW?

Barley is a short-season crop, and can be grown on either dry or irrigated land, but it prefers a cool climate. Barley is cultivated in the high mountains of Tibet and Ethiopia, the desert and coastal lands of Asia and Africa, and throughout Europe, especially in Scandinavia. In North America, barley is produced mostly in the Northern Plains states of the USA and the Western Provinces of Canada.

DIRECTIONS   :35

1. Preheat the oven to 400°F (205°C).

2. In a large mixing bowl, combine the all-purpose flour, barley flour, salt, baking soda, barley flakes, and brown sugar.

3. Cut the margarine *(or coconut oil)* into the dry ingredients.

4. Add the cranberries, banana, and lemon juice and stir until moist. Stir in the almonds.

5. On a floured surface, roll out the dough and knead until pliable. Add additional barley flour as needed if dough is too soft.

6. Roll the dough into a circle and cut it into eighths. Sprinkle the dough with cinnamon sugar if desired.

7. Place the dough on a greased baking sheet. Bake for 12–14 minutes, or until lightly browned.

Yields 8 scones.

SUGGESTIONS
Applesauce can be used instead of the banana.

ⓥ ⚜ RAISIN SCONES

You could call this a basic scone. The recipe is simple to whip up on short notice for mid-morning coffee.

INGREDIENTS

			VEGAN
45 mL	3 tbsp	sugar	
	2	eggs, beaten	flax eggs
240 mL	1 cup	all-purpose flour	
240 mL	1 cup	barley flour	
10 mL	2 tsp	baking powder	
6 mL	1½ tsp	cinnamon	
5 mL	1 tsp	baking soda	
2 mL	½ tsp	nutmeg	
2 mL	½ tsp	salt	
80 mL	⅓ cup	canola margarine	coconut oil
120 mL	½ cup	milk	soy milk
120 mL	½ cup	raisins	

IMPLEMENTS

Oven • Baking sheet • Large mixing bowl • Pastry cutter • Bread board

recipe continues on page 274 ▶

▶ **Raisin Scones,** *continued from 272.*

DIRECTIONS   *:40*

① Preheat the oven to 425°F (220°C) and grease the baking sheet.

② Reserve 1 tsp (5 mL) of the sugar.
Non-vegan: also reserve 1 tbsp (15 mL) of beaten eggs.

③ In a large bowl, combine the remaining sugar with the all-purpose flour, barley flour, baking powder, cinnamon, baking soda, nutmeg, and salt.

④ With a pastry blender, cut in the margarine *(or coconut oil)* until the mixture resembles coarse crumbs.

⑤ **Non-vegan:** Stir in the remaining eggs, the milk, and the raisins until combined.

Vegan: Stir in the flax eggs, the soy milk, and the raisins until combined.

⑥ On a lightly-floured surface, knead the dough 5 times.

⑦ Divide the dough in half and pat each half into a circle.
Cut each circle into 8 wedges.
Transfer the wedges to the baking sheet.

⑧ **Non-vegan:** Brush each wedge with the reserved beaten egg.

⑨ Sprinkle each wedge with the reserved sugar.

⑩ Bake the wedges for 17 minutes, or until browned.

Yields 16 scones.

ⓥ 🌾 APRICOT SCONES

The extra work is worth it for these oat-filled scones.

INGREDIENTS
VEGAN

360 mL	1½ cups	all-purpose flour	
120 mL	½ cup	barley flakes	
60 mL	¼ cup	sugar	
12 mL	2½ tsp	baking powder	
1 mL	¼ tsp	salt	
80 mL	⅓ cup	canola margarine	coconut oil
	2	eggs	flax eggs
60 mL	¼ cup	sour cream	

or...	60 mL	¼ cup	raw cashews
	5 mL	1 tsp	lemon juice
	5 mL	1 tsp	apple cider vinegar
	30 mL	2 tbsp	water
		pinch	salt

15 mL	1 tbsp	milk	soy milk
180 mL	¾ cup	dried apricots, chopped	
45 mL	3 tbsp	brown sugar	
15 mL	1 tbsp	quick-cooking oats	
15 mL	1 tbsp	canola margarine	coconut oil

IMPLEMENTS

Oven • Mixing bowl x2 • Small mixing bowl • Bread board
Baking sheet

recipe continues on page 276 ▶

▶ **Apricot Scones,** *continued from 275.*

DIRECTIONS   *:40*

❶ Vegan recipe only, start with step 1:
Soak the raw cashes in very hot water for 30 minutes.
Drain the cashews and blend them with the lemon juice, apple cider vinegar, 2 tbsp (30 mL) of water, and salt.
Blend until smooth, adding more water 1 tbsp (15 mL) at a time to achieve a sour-cream-like consistency.
Set the cashew mixture aside.

❷ Both recipes, continue with step 2:
Preheat the oven to 400°F (205°C).

❸ In a bowl, combine the all-purpose flour, barley flakes, sugar, baking powder, and salt.

❹ Cut the canola margarine (or coconut oil) into the flour mixture until it resembles fine crumbs.

❺ **Non-vegan:** Beat the eggs. Set aside 1 tbsp (15 mL) for the glaze.

❻ **Non-vegan:** In another bowl, combine the sour cream, milk, and the remaining beaten eggs. Add the apricots.

Vegan: In another bowl, combine the cashew mixture, soy milk, and flax eggs. Add the apricots.

7 Stir the apricot mixture into the flour mixture until mixed well.

8 On a lightly-floured surface, turn out the dough and knead it 12–15 times.

9 Divide the dough in half.
Pat one half into a circle on a greased baking sheet.

10 Combine the brown sugar, oats, and additional margarine *(or coconut oil)*.
Sprinkle the filling over the dough.

11 Roll out the remaining half of the dough into a circle.
Place the dough on the filling.
Non-vegan: Brush the top with the reserved beaten egg.
Both: Sprinkle the top with the additional sugar.

12 Cut the dough into wedges.
Bake the wedges for 15–20 minutes, or until lightly browned.

Yields 6 scones.

Ⓥ 🌾 FRUIT MINI-SCONES

Any fruit or a combination of fruits can be used for these scones. We suggest mango, cherries, golden raisins, or pineapple.

INGREDIENTS   *VEGAN*

600 mL	2½ cups	all-purpose flour	
240 mL	1 cup	flaked barley	
60 mL	¼ cup	brown sugar	
60 mL	¼ cup	sugar	
15 mL	3 tsp	baking powder	
2 mL	½ tsp	salt	
5 mL	1 tsp	cinnamon	
120 mL	½ cup	canola oil	
180 mL	¾ cup	dried fruit, diced	
180 mL	¾ cup	skim milk	soy milk

Glaze:

180 mL	¾ cup	powdered sugar	
5 mL	1 tsp	vanilla	
20 mL	4 tsp	milk	soy milk

IMPLEMENTS

Oven • Large mixing bowl • Bread board • Baking sheet
Small mixing bowl

DIRECTIONS   :35

1 Preheat the oven to 400°F (205°C).

2 In a large bowl, combine the all-purpose flour, barley, brown sugar, sugar, baking powder, salt, and cinnamon.

3 Add the oil and blend thoroughly.
Add the fruit and stir until coated.

4 Add the milk *(or soy milk)* and blend together.

5 On a floured surface, turn out the dough and knead it 5 times.

6 Divide the dough into 3 pieces.
Roll each piece into a circle and cut into 8 wedges.

7 Place the wedges on an ungreased baking sheet.
Bake at 400°F (205°C) for 12–14 minutes.

8 In a small bowl, combine the powdered sugar, vanilla, and milk *(or soy milk)*. Stir to achieve a smooth consistency.
Brush the glaze over the warm scones.

Yields 24 scones.

SUGGESTIONS
Don't forget to vary the fruits for different flavor combinations!

BANNOCKS

These bannocks are famous in the Orkney Islands, where special barley has been grown for bread baking for centuries. We had the privilege of visiting there, and saw the water-powered mill where the grain is ground into flour.

INGREDIENTS   *VEGAN*

480 mL	2 cups	**barley flour**
240 mL	1 cup	**all-purpose flour**
5 mL	1 tsp	**cream of tartar**
2 mL	½ tsp	**salt**
5 mL	1 tsp	**baking soda**
180 mL	¾ cup	**buttermilk**
or...	180 mL	¾ cup	**soy milk**
	4 mL	¾ tsp	**apple cider vinegar**

IMPLEMENTS

Griddle • Mixing bowl • Small mixing bowl

DIRECTIONS   *:30*

1 Combine the barley flour, all-purpose flour, cream of tartar, and salt.

2 In a small bowl, stir together the baking soda and buttermilk *(or soy milk and apple cider vinegar)*.

3 Combine the two mixtures and mix to create a dough.
If needed, add extra buttermlik *(or soy milk and apple cider vinegar, in proportion)* to achieve a moist dough.
Form the dough into a ball.

4 On a lightly-floured surface, roll the dough out to about ½" (1 cm) thick.
Cut the dough into circles about 4" (10 cm) in diameter.

5 Place the bannocks on a hot, ungreased griddle.
Bake for 5 minutes on each side, or until the center is cooked.

Yields 12 bannocks

ⓥ 🌾 CINNAMON SWEET BISCUITS

Who can resist the flavour of cinnamon?

INGREDIENTS

			VEGAN
480 mL	2 cups	barley flour	
240 mL	1 cup	all-purpose flour	
120 mL	½ cup	sugar	
15 mL	1 tbsp	baking powder	
2 mL	½ tsp	salt	
180 mL	¾ cup	canola margarine	coconut oil
	2	eggs	flax eggs
120 mL	½ cup	milk	soy milk
60 mL	¼ cup	brown sugar	
3 mL	½ tsp	cinnamon	
120 mL	½ cup	raisins	

IMPLEMENTS

Oven • Muffin pan • Mixing bowls: small x2, medium • Bread board

DID YOU KNOW?

The *dietary fiber* in barley helps keep digestion moving and gives fuel to helpful micro-organisms in our intestines. Increasing the amount of dietary fiber that you eat can help prevent constipation and diverticulitis.

DIRECTIONS   :40

❶ Preheat the oven to 375°F (190°C).

❷ Combine the barley flour, all-purpose flour, sugar, baking powder, and salt.

❸ Cut the margarine *(or coconut oil)* into the flour mixture.

❹ **Non-vegan:** In a small bowl, beat the eggs and stir in the milk.
Vegan: In a small bowl, mix the flax eggs and the soy milk.

❺ Add the egg mixture to the flour mixture and blend together well.

❻ On a floured surface, roll the dough into a rectangle.

❼ In a small bowl, combine the sugar and cinnamon.
Sprinkle the sugar and cinnamon over the dough rectangle.
Sprinkle the raisins over the top.

❽ Roll the dough into a tube shape.
Slice the tube into 12 biscuits.
Place each biscuit in a muffin tin.

❾ Bake the biscuits for 15–20 minutes, or until lightly browned.

Yields 12 biscuits.

SUGGESTIONS

For a sweeter treat, drizzle thin white frosting over the biscuits while they're still warm.

ⓥ 🌾 ANGEL BISCUITS

A unique, lighter biscuit. Recipe from Sandy Schmitt.

INGREDIENTS   *VEGAN*

15 mL	1 tbsp	active dry yeast	
120 mL	½ cup	warm water	
720 mL	2½ cups	all-purpose flour	
480 mL	2 cups	barley flour	
5 mL	1 tsp	baking powder	
5 mL	1 tsp	baking soda	
5 mL	1 tsp	salt	
45 mL	3 tbsp	sugar	
180 mL	¾ cup	canola margarine	coconut oil
480 mL	2 cups	buttermilk	

or...	480 mL	2 cups	soy milk
	10 mL	2 tsp	apple cider vinegar

IMPLEMENTS

Oven • Small mixing bowl • Large mixing bowl • Baking sheet

DIRECTIONS   :30

1. Preheat the oven to 400°F (205°C).

2. In a small bowl, dissolve the yeast in warm water.

3. In a large bowl, combine the all-purpose flour, barley flour, baking powder, baking soda, salt, and sugar.

4. Cut the margarine *(or coconut oil)* into the flour mixture.

5. Blend the buttermilk *(or soy milk and apple cider vinegar)* and the yeast.

6. Combine the flour mixture and the yeast mixture.

7. Drop the dough, one spoonful at a time, onto the baking sheet.

8. Bake for 10–12 minutes, or until lightly brown.

Yields 18 biscuits.
This is a big batch, but the biscuits keep well.

DID YOU KNOW?

Fats have other purposes aside from storing energy. Barley contains a relatively low level of fat, but some of the fatty acids in barley are involved in critical processes in our bodies.

Ⓥ 🌾 BARLEY BISCUITS

A low-calorie recipe with no cholesterol content.

INGREDIENTS

VEGAN

240 mL	1 cup	barley flour	
240 mL	1 cup	all-purpose flour	
6 mL	1¼ tsp	baking powder	
5 mL	1 tsp	salt	
60 mL	¼ cup	canola margarine	coconut oil
60 mL	½ cup	milk	soy milk

IMPLEMENTS

Oven • Mixing bowl • Pastry cutter • Bread board • Baking sheet

DID YOU KNOW?

In 2012, a study showed that the *beta-glucans* found in barley can significantly decrease blood cholesterol. Your liver is key to how this works.

Normally, your liver uses cholesterol to produce *bile acids*, which help digest food and are then re-absorbed by your intestines. When you eat beta-glucans, a gel forms in your small intenstine that makes it harder to re-absorb the bile acids.

This forces your liver to create more bile acids, which uses more cholesterol, pulling the cholesterol out of your bloodstream. In addition, some of the dietary fat that you've eaten is prevented from being absorbed by the same gel.

DIRECTIONS   *:35*

❶ Preheat the oven to 450°F (230°C).

❷ Mix together the barley flour, all-purpose flour, baking powder, and salt.

❸ Using a pastry cutter, cut the margarine *(or coconut oil)* into the mixture until it resembles coarse crumbs.

❹ Add the milk *(or soy milk)* to the mixture.
Using a fork, mix just until the mixture leaves the sides of the bowl.

❺ Turn the dough out onto a lightly floured bread board.
Knead for 8–10 strokes to mix the dough thoroughly.

❻ Pat the dough flat until about ½" (1 cm) thick.

❼ Cut the dough into biscuits.
Place the biscuits on an ungreased baking sheet.
Bake for 12–15 minutes, or until lightly brown.

Yields 8–10 biscuits.

SUGGESTIONS

You can also start with a biscuit mix and add a little barley flour or flaked barley. If you do, add a bit more baking powder and liquid.

❦ DESSERTS ❦

pictured: Peach Pecan Crisp, page 352

DESSERTS

Cookies

		Time	Barley
294 v	Molasses Cookies	:30	flour
296 v	Barley Flake Cookies	:30	flour
298 v	Snickerdoodles	1:00	flour
300 v	Walnut Butter Cookies	:35	flour
302 v	Peanut Butter Cookies	:30	flour
304 v	Korean Sesame Seed Cookies	1:35	flour
306 v	Caraway Cookies	:25	flour
308 v	Anisette Stars	:45	flour
311 v	Almond Shortbread	:35	flour

Cakes

312 v	Linzer Torte	1:10	flour
314 v	Rhubarb Cake	1:10	flour
316 v	Carrot Loaf Cake	1:25	flour
318	Chocolate Cake	1:15	flour
320 v	Chocolate Zucchini Cake	1:10	flour
322	Streusel Cake	:55	flour
324 v	Orange Coffee Cake	:50	flour

Calories	Balance			g Fat	g Prot	g Carb	g Fiber	mg Chol
	F	P	C					
110	●	·	●	4	1	18	1 ·	10 ●
100	●	·	●	4	2	15	1 ·	10 ●
90	●	·	●	3	1	13	1 ·	10 ●
80	●		·	6	1	8	1 ·	5 ●
110	●	·	·	5	3	14	1 ·	10 ●
70	●	·	·	4	2	8	1 ●	5 ·
110	●	·	●	5	1	12	1 ·	15 ●
110	·	·	●	3	3	19	1 ·	25 ●
270	●	·	·	16	5	27	3 ·	13 ·
500	●	·	·	27	7	61	4 ·	60 ●
350	●	·	●	13	5	56	3 ·	20 ·
360	●	·	●	17	5	49	2 ·	55 ●
500	●	·	●	21	6	77	2 -	55 ●
280	●	·	●	11	3	44	2 ·	30 ●
330	●	·	●	15	5	47	3 ·	70 ●
370	·	·	●	9	6	67	3 ·	30 ·

ᐱ DESSERTS CONTINUED

Brownies, Bars, and Squares		Time	Barley
326	Coconut Brownies	:55	flour
328 V	Toll House Squares	:30	flour
330 V	Fig Bars	1:20	flour
332	Lemon Squares	1:05	flour
334 V	Pumpkin Pie Bars	1:25	flour+flakes
336 V	Carrot Bars	:50	flakes
338 V	Zucchini Bars	:40	flakes
340 V	Chocolate Peanut Squares	1:20	flour

Puddings and Custards			
344 V	Quick Barley Pudding	1:00	pearl
345	Barley Rice Custard	1:55	pearl
346	Toasted Barley Meringue Pudding	1:10	flakes
348 V	Apple Pudding	1:25	quick
350 V	Krentje Brij	4:25	pearl

Other Desserts			
351 V	Apple Crisp	:55	flour+flakes
352 V	Peach Pecan Crisp	:55	flour
354 V	Scottish Apple Buns	:45	flour

Calories	Balance F	P	C	g Fat	g Prot	g Carb	g Fiber	mg Chol
260	●	•	•	17	3	27	2 •	30 ●
360	●	•	•	22	5	42	3 •	35 •
90	•	•	●	2	1	17	1 ●	0 -
190	●	•	●	8	2	28	2 ●	35 ●
210	●	•	•	11	4	27	3 ●	20 •
240	•	•	●	6	4	44	4 ●	20 •
160	●	•	●	7	2	24	1 •	20 ●
240	●	•	•	13	5	30	2 •	15 •
190	●	•	●	9	4	25	2 •	5 •
300	•	•	●	5	10	53	4 •	130 ◉
230	•	•	●	5	9	39	2 •	100 ◉
170	-	-	◉	0	1	44	3 ●	0 -
180	-	•	◉	0	2	46	4 ●	0 -
230	•	-	●	8	2	40	4 ●	0 -
270	●	•	•	13	3	41	4 ●	15 •
300	•	•	●	9	6	52	4 ●	30 •

Ⓥ 🌾 MOLASSES COOKIES

These cookies are reminiscent of times past.

INGREDIENTS   *VEGAN*

120 mL	½ cup	canola margarine			coconut oil
120 mL	½ cup	butter			
		or...	150 mL	10 tbsp	coconut oil (room temp.)
			60 mL	¼ cup	soy milk
			5 mL	1 tsp	apple cider vinegar
			2 mL	½ tsp	sea salt
240 mL	1 cup	sugar			
	1	egg			flax egg
240 mL	1 cup	molasses			
180 mL	¾ cup	hot water			
480 mL	2 cups	barley flour			
480 mL	2 cups	all-purpose flour			
5 mL	1 tsp	cinnamon			
5 mL	1 tsp	ginger			
10 mL	2 tsp	baking soda			
1 mL	¼ tsp	salt			

IMPLEMENTS

Oven • Baking sheet • Large mixing bowl • Sieve

DIRECTIONS *:30*

1 Preheat the oven to 350°F (175°C).

2 **Vegan:** Mix the coconut oil, soy milk, apple cider vinegar, and sea salt. Blend for 2 minutes.

3 In a large bowl, combine the margarine, butter, sugar, eggs, molasses, and hot water. The hot water can be used to rinse the molasses out of the cup.

4 Sift together the barley and all-purpose flour then add to the molasses. Add the cinnamon, ginger, baking soda and salt. Mix together until well-blended. More flour may be added gradually until the batter is thick.

5 Drop heaping spoonfuls of the dough onto a greased cookie sheet.

6 Bake for 10–15 minutes.

Yields 48 cookies.

SUGGESTIONS
Try frosting these cookies with white icing!

ⓥ 🌾 BARLEY FLAKE COOKIES

These cookies are comparable to traditional oatmeal cookies.

INGREDIENTS   *VEGAN*

180 mL	¾ cup	canola margarine	coconut oil
120 mL	½ cup	sugar	
120 mL	½ cup	brown sugar	
	2	eggs	flax eggs
120 mL	½ cup	milk	soy milk
5 mL	1 tsp	vanilla	
480 mL	2 cups	barley flour	
5 mL	1 tsp	baking powder	
5 mL	1 tsp	cinnamon	
3 mL	½ tsp	cloves	
5 mL	1 tsp	nutmeg	
240 mL	1 cup	raisins	
120 mL	½ cup	nuts, chopped	
480 mL	2 cups	barley flakes	

IMPLEMENTS

Oven • Baking sheet(s) • Large mixing bowl • Sieve • Cooling rack(s)

DIRECTIONS   :30

❶ Preheat the oven to 350°F (175°C).

❷ In a large mixing bowl, combine the margarine *(or coconut oil)*, sugar, brown sugar, eggs *(or flax eggs)*, milk *(or soy milk)*, and vanilla.

❸ Sift 1 cup (240 mL) of the barley flour, along with the baking powder, cinnamon, cloves, and nutmeg into the moist ingredients.

❹ Add the remaining flour, the raisins, and the nuts.
Blend together.
Mix in the barley flakes.

❺ Drop heaping spoonfuls of the dough onto a greased cookie sheet.

❻ Bake for 12–15 minutes and cool on a cooling rack.

Yields 48 cookies.

ⓥ 🌾 SNICKERDOODLES

This is a healthier version of an old favorite.

INGREDIENTS   *VEGAN*

120 mL	½ cup	**canola margarine**			
		or...	180 mL	¾ cup	**coconut oil**
60 mL	¼ cup	**butter**			*(leave out butter)*
360 mL	1½ cups	**sugar**			
	2	**eggs**		1	**banana**, mashed
480 mL	2 cups	**barley flour**			
180 mL	¾ cup	**all-purpose flour**			
10 mL	2 tsp	**cream of tartar**			
5 mL	1 tsp	**baking soda**			
1 mL	¼ tsp	**salt**			
10 mL	2 tsp	**cinnamon**			
60 mL	¼ cup	**sugar**			

IMPLEMENTS

Oven • Baking sheet(s) • Mixing bowl x2

DID YOU KNOW?

Barley and other plant seeds contain high levels of the mineral *phosphorus*. However, 75% or more of plant phosphorus is locked in an indigestible form called *phytic acid*.

DIRECTIONS

❶ Preheat the oven to 350°F (175°C).

❷ **Non-vegan:** Cream together the margarine, butter, 1½ cups (360 mL) of sugar, and the eggs.

Vegan: Cream together the coconut oil, 1½ cups (360 mL) of sugar, and the mashed banana.

❸ In a separate bowl, sift together the flour, cream of tartar, baking soda, and salt. Add this dry mixture to the creamed mixture.

❹ Chill the dough for 30 minutes.

❺ Shape the dough into balls with your hands, using about 1 tsp (5mL) of the dough for each ball. (Each one should be the size of a walnut). If the dough feels sticky when forming the balls, add a little more wheat flour.

❻ Roll the balls in a mixture of the cinnamon and ¼ cup (60 mL) of sugar.

❼ Place the balls on ungreased cookie sheets, about 2" (5 cm) apart.

❽ Bake for 10–12 minutes.

Yields 48 cookies.

ⓥ 🌾 WALNUT BUTTER COOKIES

A rich, tasty cookie with potential for variations.

INGREDIENTS

VEGAN

120 mL	½ cup	canola margarine			
	or...	240 mL	1 cup	coconut oil	
120 mL	½ cup	butter		*(leave out butter)*	
120 mL	½ cup	sugar			
	1	egg yolk		1	flax egg *
5 mL	1 tsp	vanilla			
1 mL	¼ tsp	salt			
2 mL	½ tsp	baking powder			
240 mL	1 cup	barley flour			
240 mL	1 cup	all-purpose flour			
480 mL	2 cups	walnuts, finely chopped			
240 mL	1 cup	powdered sugar			

* (make with only 1 tbsp / 15mL of water)

IMPLEMENTS

Oven • Baking sheet(s) • Mixing bowl

DIRECTIONS   :35

1. Preheat the oven to 300°F (150°C).

2. **Non-vegan:** Cream together the margarine, butter, sugar, egg yolk, and vanilla until the mixture is fluffy.

   Vegan: Cream together the coconut oil, sugar, flax egg, and vanilla until the mixture is fluffy.

3. Sift the salt, baking powder, and flour into the creamed mixture. Add the chopped walnuts and mix together until well-blended.

4. Shape the dough into balls the size of whole walnuts and place them on a lightly greased cookie sheet.

5. Bake for 12–15 minutes.

6. **Non-vegan:** Roll the cookies in powdered sugar while still hot.
   Vegan: Sprinkle powdered sugar over the cookies while still hot.

Yields 60 cookies.

SUGGESTIONS
Try pecans or other nuts in place of the walnuts.

PEANUT BUTTER COOKIES

The chopped peanuts add a unique flavor and texture to these healthy cookies.

INGREDIENTS   *VEGAN*

120 mL	½ cup	**all-purpose flour**				
240 mL	1 cup	**barley flour**				
160 mL	⅔ cup	**peanuts**, chopped				
7 mL	1½ tsp	**baking soda**				
120 mL	½ cup	**canola margarine**				
		or...	240 mL	1 cup	**coconut oil**	
120 mL	½ cup	**butter**			*(leave out butter)*	
480 mL	2 cups	**brown sugar**				
240 mL	1 cup	**peanut butter**				
	2	**eggs**			**flax eggs**	
5 mL	1 tsp	**vanilla**				
3 mL	½ tsp	**ground nutmeg**				
360 mL	1½ cups	**barley flakes**				

IMPLEMENTS

Oven • Electric mixer • Large and medium mixing bowls
Baking sheet • Cooling rack

DIRECTIONS :30

1. Preheat the oven to 375°F (190°C).

2. In a medium mixing bowl, stir together the all-purpose flour, barley flour, chopped peanuts, and baking soda.

3. In a larger bowl, using an electric mixer, beat the margarine and butter *(or the coconut oil)* on medium speed until softened.

4. Add the brown sugar, peanut butter, eggs *(or flax eggs)*, vanilla, and nutmeg to the wet mixture and beat well.

5. Add the flour mixture to the wet mixture and beat on low speed until combined.

6. Shape the dough into small balls and roll them in the barley flakes.

7. Place the balls on a greased cookie sheet 2" (5 cm) apart.
   Flatten each ball with the bottom of a glass.

8. Bake for 8–10 minutes.

9. Cool on a wire rack.

Yields 60 cookies.

KOREAN SESAME SEED COOKIES

Korean cuisine has a history of using barley. These unique cookies are delicious and not too sweet. They are nice with a glass of wine or a cup of green tea!

INGREDIENTS

VEGAN

120 mL	½ cup	sesame seeds	
540 mL	2¼ cups	barley flour	
5 mL	1 tsp	baking powder	
1 mL	¼ tsp	salt	
120 mL	½ cup	butter	coconut oil
180 mL	¾ cup	sugar	
	1	egg	flax egg
30 mL	2 tbsp	cold water	

IMPLEMENTS

Oven • Pie plate • Mixing bowl x2 • Sieve • Aluminum foil
Baking sheet(s)

DID YOU KNOW?

The planned landing site for the Mayflower was originally much further south than Plymouth Rock, but was changed due to a shortage of beer!

In the 1600's, it was very difficult to keep water safe for consumption on a long sea voyage. Beer (made, of course, with barley) remained safe to drink for long periods, and so it was the drink of choice for sailors and passengers of all ages.

DIRECTIONS   *1:35*

❶ Preheat the oven to 325°F (165°C).

❷ Spread the sesame seeds on a pie plate and toast them in the oven for 15 minutes, or until golden-brown and fragrant.
Remove the seeds and set them aside to cool.
Turn off the oven.

❸ Sift together the flour, baking powder, and salt. Set aside.

❹ In a mixing bowl, cream the butter *(or coconut oil)* until softened.

❺ Add the sugar, egg *(or flax egg)*, and ⅓ cup (80 mL) of the sesame seeds.
Blend well.

❻ Add the flour mixture and water to the sesame seed mixture. Alternate between adding some of the flour, then a little of the water. Mix well.

❼ Shape the dough into an oblong roll about 10" (25 cm) long.
Wrap the dough roll in foil and chill for 1 hour.

🕐   *... after 1 hour ...*

❽ Preheat the oven to 350°F (175°C).

❾ Cut the dough into ⅛" (3 mm) slices and place the slices on greased cookie sheets.

❿ Sprinkle the cookies with the remaining sesame seeds.
Press the seeds down into the dough.

⓫ Bake for 12–15 minutes.

Yields 40 cookies.

⊙ ❖ CARAWAY COOKIES

This was one of my mother's recipes, adapted to include barley—one of my favorites and not too sweet.

INGREDIENTS

VEGAN

120 mL	½ cup	canola margarine	coconut oil
180 mL	¾ cup	sugar	
	2	eggs	flax eggs
5 mL	1 tsp	vanilla	
80 mL	⅓ cup	water	
15 mL	1 tbsp	caraway seeds	
300 mL	1¼ cups	barley flour	
240 mL	1 cup	all-purpose flour	
5 mL	1 tsp	baking powder	
5 mL	1 tsp	salt	

IMPLEMENTS

Oven • Mixing bowl • Sieve • Baking sheet(s)

DID YOU KNOW?

As far back as ancient times, heat exhaustion, fever, and intestinal irritation have been treated by frequently drinking barley water (water in which barley was boiled). More recently, barley water has been used to ease the side effects of chemotherapy.

Little research has been done on barley water, and most claims are only anecdotes, rather than clinical evidence. However, we (the authors) have witnessed these phenomena and are convinced of the benefits of barley water. See page 358 for instructions to make barley water.

DIRECTIONS   :25

❶ Preheat the oven to 325°F (165°C).

❷ Cream the margarine *(or coconut oil)* until softened.

❸ Gradually mix in the sugar.

❹ Add the eggs *(or flax eggs)* and beat until smooth.

❺ Add the vanilla, water, and caraway seeds and mix together.

❻ Sift the barley flour, all-purpose flour, baking powder, and salt together into the batter and mix until smooth.

❼ Drop the batter 1 tsp (5 ml) at a time onto a greased baking sheet.

❽ Bake for 10 minutes, or until firm.

Yields 24 cookies.

ⓥ 🌾 ANISETTE STARS

An adaptation of my mother's original recipe. The anise flavor and star-like shape make these cookies unique.

INGREDIENTS   *VEGAN*

480 mL	2 cups	**barley flour**	
240 mL	1 cup	**all-purpose flour**	
12 mL	2½ tsp	**baking powder**	
1 mL	¼ tsp	**baking soda**	
2 mL	½ tsp	**salt**	
60 mL	¼ cup	**canola margarine**	coconut oil
120 mL	½ cup	**sugar**	
	3	**eggs**	flax eggs
30 mL	2 tbsp	**anise seeds**	
5 mL	1 tsp	**lemon peel**, grated	
25 mL	1½ tbsp	**lemon juice**	
5 mL	1 tsp	**vanilla**	
30 mL	2 tbsp	**sugar**	

IMPLEMENTS

Oven • Mixing bowl x2 • Bread board • Baking sheet(s)

recipe continues on page 310 ▶

▶ **Anisette Stars,** *continued from 308.*

DIRECTIONS   :45

1 Preheat the oven to 350°F (175°C).

2 Combine the barley flour, all-purpose flour, baking powder, baking soda, and salt. Set aside.

3 Cream together the margarine *(or coconut oil)* and ½ cup (120 mL) sugar.

4 Add the eggs *(or flax eggs)* to the mixture and beat until creamy.

5 Stir in the anise seed, lemon peel, lemon juice, and vanilla.

6 Gradually blend the flour mixture into the wet mixture to form a stiff, well-blended dough.

7 Knead the dough on a lightly-floured board until smooth.

8 Divide the dough into eight equal parts.
Roll each part by hand into a strip about ½" (1 cm) thick.
Cut each strip into 4" (10 cm) pieces.

9 Along the edge of each piece, every ½" (1 cm), cut a slit halfway through.

10 Press the ends of each piece together in a circle, with the slits facing out.

11 Place the stars on a greased cookie sheet.
Sprinkle the remaining 2 tbsp (30 mL) of sugar over the cookies.

12 Bake for 15 minutes.

Yields 24 cookies.

SUGGESTIONS
Add chopped candied cherries for a festive twist.

ⓥ 🌾 ALMOND SHORTBREAD

These cookies are not too sweet, nice with a cup of hot anything.

INGREDIENTS   *VEGAN*

180 mL	¾ cup	**canola margarine**			
	or...		150 mL	10 tbsp	**coconut oil** (room temp.)
			60 mL	¼ cup	**soy milk**
			5 mL	1 tsp	**apple cider vinegar**
			2 mL	½ tsp	**sea salt**
120 mL	½ cup	**butter**			**canola oil**
300 mL	1¼ cups	**powdered sugar**			
240 mL	1 cup	*each:* **barley flour, all-purpose flour**, and **whole wheat flour**			
480 mL	2 cups	**slivered almonds**			

IMPLEMENTS

Oven • Large mixing bowl • Two baking pans, 8"x8" (20x20 cm)

DIRECTIONS   :35

❶ Preheat the oven to 350°F (175°C).

❷ **Vegan:** Blend together the margarine substitute ingredients for 2 minutes.

❸ In a large mixing bowl, cream together the margarine (or coconut oil mixture), butter (or canola oil), and powdered sugar.

❹ Mix in the barley, all-purpose, and whole wheat flours until well-blended. Stir in the slivered almonds until all are coated in the batter.

❺ Press the mixture into two 8"x8" (20x20 cm) baking pans.
Bake for 20–25 minutes.
Allow to cool partially. Cut into bars while still slightly warm.

Yields 18 shortbreads.

ⓥ 🌾 LINZER TORTE

A famous German dessert, great for special occasions.

INGREDIENTS   *VEGAN*

240 mL	1 cup	sugar	
60 mL	¼ cup	unsalted butter	coconut oil
120 mL	½ cup	canola oil	
5 mL	1 tsp	lemon peel, grated	
	2	eggs	flax eggs
180 mL	¾ cup	barley flour	
180 mL	¾ cup	all-purpose flour	
240 mL	1 cup	ground almonds	
3 mL	½ tsp	cinnamon	
1 mL	¼ tsp	nutmeg	
30 mL	2 tbsp	cocoa	
1 mL	¼ tsp	salt	
120 mL	½ cup	raspberry jam	

IMPLEMENTS

Oven • Electric mixer • Mixing bowl • Grater/Zester • Wax paper
Pie pan, shallow

DID YOU KNOW?

Caffe d'orzo (coffee of barley) is an Italian drink made from ground roasted barley. Caffe d'orzo is substituted for coffee for health reasons in Italy.

DIRECTIONS

1. Preheat the oven to 400°F (205°C).

2. With an electric mixer, beat together the sugar, butter *(or coconut oil)*, and canola oil until light and creamy.

3. Stir in the lemon peel.

4. Add one egg *(or flax egg)*, then beat thoroughly.
   Repeat with the other egg *(or flax egg)*.

5. Add the barley flour, all-purpose flour, almonds, cinnamon, nutmeg, cocoa, and salt to the dough. Beat until fluffy.

6. Divide the dough in half.
   Roll one portion of the dough between two sheets of waxed paper.

7. Place the rolled dough into a shallow pie pan.
   Spread the jam over the dough.

8. Roll out the remaining dough and cut it into strips.
   Place the strips over the jam to form a lattice.

9. Bake for 30–40 minutes, or until slightly brown.

Yields 8 servings.

SUGGESTIONS

If the dough is sticky, chill it for a while and it will become easier to handle.

If desired, sprinkle powdered sugar over the top of the torte after it has been baked and cooled.

Ⓥ ❦ RHUBARB CAKE

This cake has been a hit with all tasters. If you freeze sliced rhubarb, you can make this cake any time you like.

INGREDIENTS

			VEGAN
120 mL	½ cup	canola margarine	coconut oil
360 mL	1½ cups	sugar	
	1	egg	flax egg
240 mL	1 cup	buttermilk	
	or...	240 mL	1 cup soy milk
		5 mL	1 tsp apple cider vinegar
360 mL	1½ cups	barley flour	
360 mL	1½ cups	all-purpose flour, divided	
5 mL	1 tsp	baking soda	
5 mL	1 tsp	salt	
5 mL	1 tsp	vanilla	
60 mL	¼ cup	orange juice	
	1	orange peel, grated	
720 mL	2½ cups	rhubarb, chopped	
180 mL	¾ cup	brown sugar	
180 mL	¾ cup	chopped nuts	
5 mL	1 tsp	cinnamon	
60 mL	¼ cup	butter, melted	coconut oil, melted

IMPLEMENTS

Oven • Mixing bowls: large, small ×2 • Grater/Zester
Baking pan, 9"x13" (23x33 cm)

DIRECTIONS   *1:10*

1 Preheat the oven to 350°F (175°C).

2 In a large mixing bowl, cream together the margarine *(or coconut oil)* and the sugar.

3 **Non-vegan:** Add the egg and buttermilk.
Vegan: Add the flax egg, soy milk, and apple cider vinegar.

4 Mix until well-blended.

5 In a small bowl, combine the barley flour, 1 cup (240 mL) of the all-purpose flour, the baking soda, and the salt.

6 Combine the two mixtures in the large bowl and mix until well-blended.

7 Stir in the vanilla, orange juice, and orange peel.

8 Add the rhubarb and mix until it's well-coated.

9 Pour the batter into a greased, 9"x13" (23x33 cm) baking pan.

10 In a small bowl, combine the brown sugar, remaining all-purpose flour, nuts, cinnamon, and melted butter *(or melted coconut oil)*.

11 Sprinkle the nut mix over top of the batter in the pan.

12 Bake for 45 minutes.

Yields 15 servings.

CARROT LOAF CAKE

This luscious cake does not demand to be frosted, but the cream cheese topping does add a nice touch.

INGREDIENTS

			VEGAN
180 mL	¾ cup	**canola margarine**	coconut oil
225 g	8 oz	**light cream cheese**	

		or...	225 g	8 oz	**firm silken tofu**
			15 mL	1 tbsp	**lemon juice**
			5 mL	1 tsp	**sea salt**
			2 mL	½ tsp	**sugar**

360 mL	1½ cups	**sugar**	
	4	**eggs**	flax eggs
480 mL	2 cups	**carrots**, shredded	
240 mL	1 cup	**pecans**, finely chopped	
225 g	8 oz	**canned crushed pineapple**, drained	
240 mL	1 cup	**all-purpose flour**	
360 mL	1½ cups	**barley flour**	
15 mL	1 tbsp	**baking powder**	
15 mL	1 tbsp	**lemon peel**	
2 mL	½ tsp	**salt**	
60 mL	¼ cup	**butter**, softened	coconut butter
5 mL	1 tsp	**vanilla**	
660 mL	2¾ cups	**powdered sugar**	

IMPLEMENTS

Oven • Large and medium mixing bowls
Two loaf pans, both 8"x4"x2" (20x10x5 cm)

DIRECTIONS   *1:25*

1 Preheat the oven to 350°F (175°C).

2 **Vegan:** Combine the tofu, lemon juice, sea salt, and sugar.
Blend until smooth.

3 In a large mixing bowl, cream together the margarine *(or coconut oil)* along with 4 oz (110 g) of the cream cheese *(or tofu mixture)*.

4 Add the sugar and beat until fluffy.

5 Beat in the eggs *(or flax eggs)*, one at a time, until combined.

6 Add the carrots, pecans, and pineapple. Stir together until blended.

7 In a separate bowl, combine the all-purpose flour, barley flour, baking powder, lemon peel and salt.
Add to the carrot mixture and mix until thoroughly blended.

8 Divide the batter into two greased 8"x4"x2" (20x10x5 cm) loaf pans.

9 Bake for 50–55 minutes, or until an inserted toothpick comes out clean.

10 To make the frosting, beat together the remaining cream cheese *(or tofu mixture)*, the butter *(or coconut butter)*, and the vanilla until fluffy.

11 Gradually beat in the powdered sugar to achieve a spreadable consistency. Spread the frosting over the cooled loaves.

Yields 20 slices.

SUGGESTIONS
For a different flavour, add some pineapple slices on top of the cake.

CHOCOLATE CAKE

This is a luxurious cake, especially with the frosting. The recipe is adapted from one made by our friend Hilary Johnson. Save it for special occasions, it's rich!

INGREDIENTS

240 mL	1 cup	boiling water
85 g	3 oz	unsweetened chocolate
60 mL	4 tbsp	butter
60 mL	4 tbsp	canola margarine
5 mL	1 tsp	vanilla
480 mL	2 cups	sugar
	2	eggs, separated
5 mL	1 tsp	baking soda
120 mL	½ cup	light sour cream
240 mL	1 cup	all-purpose flour
240 mL	1 cup	barley flour
5 mL	1 tsp	baking powder

frosting:

30 mL	2 tbsp	butter
180 mL	¾ cup	semisweet chocolate chips
90 mL	6 tbsp	heavy cream
300 mL	1¼ cups	powdered sugar
5 mL	1 tsp	vanilla

IMPLEMENTS

Oven • Mixing bowls: small x2, medium, and large • Whisk • Sieve
Tube pan, 10" (25 cm)

DIRECTIONS

1:15

1. Preheat the oven to 350°F (175°C).

2. In a large mixing bowl, combine the boiling water, chocolate, 4 tbsp (60 mL) of butter, and margarine. Allow the mixture to melt.

3. Stir in the vanilla and sugar.

4. Whisk in the egg yolks, one at a time, blending well after each one.

5. In a small bowl, combine the baking soda and sour cream. Whisk into the chocolate mixture.

6. In a small bowl, sift together the all-purpose flour, barley flour, and baking powder. Add this mixture to the batter, mixing thoroughly.

7. In a separate bowl, beat the egg whites until stiff.

8. Stir a quarter of the egg whites thoroughly into the batter.

9. Scoop the remaining egg whites on top of the batter and gently fold together.

10. Pour the batter into a greased and floured 10" (25 cm) tube pan.

11. Bake on the middle rack for 40–50 minutes.

12. To make the frosting, combine 2 tbsp (30 mL) butter, chocolate chips, heavy cream, powdered sugar, and vanilla in a pot.
    Whisk the mixture together over low heat until smooth.
    Remove the mixture from the heat and let it cool slightly.

13. After the cake has baked, remove it from the pan and allow it to cool completely, then frost it.

Yields 12 slices.

CHOCOLATE ZUCCHINI CAKE

What a delicious way to eat vegetables! When you have extra garden zucchini you can shred them and freeze them ahead of time to use in this recipe. Thanks to Judy Watson.

INGREDIENTS   *VEGAN*

240 mL	1 cup	**barley flour**			
240 mL	1 cup	**all-purpose flour**			
5 mL	1 tsp	**baking soda**			
5 mL	1 tsp	**baking powder**			
5 mL	1 tsp	**cinnamon**			
3 mL	½ tsp	**nutmeg**			
60 mL	¼ cup	**unsweetened powdered cocoa**			
	3	**eggs**			**flax eggs**
480 mL	2 cups	**sugar**			
120 mL	½ cup	**canola oil**			
180 mL	¾ cup	**buttermilk**			
	or...		180 mL	¾ cup	**soy milk**
			4 mL	¾ tsp	**apple cider vinegar**
480 mL	2 cups	**zucchini**, shredded			
5 mL	1 tsp	**vanilla**			
10 mL	2 tsp	**orange peel**, grated			
240 mL	1 cup	**chopped nuts**			
240 mL	1 cup	**powdered sugar**			
30 mL	2 tbsp	**orange juice**			

IMPLEMENTS

Oven • Mixing bowls: large, medium, and small • Sieve • Grater/Zester Baking pan, 9"x13" (23x33 cm)

DIRECTIONS

1:10

1. Preheat the oven to 350°F (175°C).

2. In a medium bowl, sift together the barley flour, all-purpose flour, baking soda, baking powder, cinnamon, nutmeg, and cocoa.

3. **Non-vegan:** In a large bowl, beat the eggs until light yellow and slightly thickened.

   Vegan: In a large bowl, briefly beat the flax eggs.

4. Add the sugar and oil slowly, while continuing to beat the egg mixture.

5. Alternately add the buttermilk *(or soy milk mixed with apple cider vinegar)* and the flour mixture to the egg mixture, stirring.

6. Stir in the zucchini, vanilla, 1 tsp (5 mL) of the orange peel, and the nuts.

7. Pour the batter into a greased and floured 9"x13" (23x33 cm) baking pan.

8. Bake for 40–45 minutes.

9. To make the glaze, combine the powdered sugar, orange juice, and remaining orange peel. Mix until well-blended (the glaze should be thin).

10. Drizzle the glaze over top of the cake while it's still hot.

Yields 18 servings.

STREUSEL CAKE

Good for breakfast or with a between-meals cup of coffee.

INGREDIENTS

60 mL	¼ cup	butter
120 mL	½ cup	sugar
	1	egg
360 mL	1½ cups	barley flour
10 mL	2 tsp	baking powder
2 mL	½ tsp	salt
120 mL	½ cup	milk
	1	egg yolk
30 mL	2 tbsp	cream
120 mL	½ cup	brown sugar
45 mL	3 tbsp	all-purpose flour
45 mL	3 tbsp	butter
5 mL	1 tsp	cinnamon
120 mL	½ cup	chopped nuts

IMPLEMENTS

Oven • Mixing bowls: medium ×2, small ×2
Baking pan, 9"×9" (23×23 cm)

DIRECTIONS

1. Preheat the oven to 375°F (190°C).

2. In a mixing bowl, cream together the butter and sugar.
   Add the egg and mix until blended.

3. In another bowl, sift together the barley flour, baking powder, and salt.

4. Alternately add the flour mixture and the milk to the creamed mixture.

5. Pour the batter into a 9"x9" (23x23 cm) greased pan.

6. Blend together the egg yolk and the 2 tbsp (30 mL) of cream.
   Pour this mixture evenly over the batter.

7. In a small mixing bowl, blend the brown sugar, all-purpose flour,
   cinnamon, margarine, and nuts to create the topping.

8. Sprinkle the topping over the batter.

9. Bake for 30 minutes.

Yields 9 servings.

ⓥ 🌾 ORANGE COFFEE CAKE

This luscious cake does not demand to be frosted, but the crumbly topping does add a nice touch.

INGREDIENTS   *VEGAN*

240 mL	1 cup	barley flour	
480 mL	2 cups	all-purpose flour	
2 mL	½ tsp	salt	
120 mL	½ cup	sugar	
20 mL	4 tsp	baking powder	
15 mL	1 tbsp	orange peel, grated	
60 mL	¼ cup	canola margarine	coconut oil
	1	egg	flax egg
150 mL	10 tbsp	orange juice	
120 mL	½ cup	milk	soy milk
180 mL	¾ cup	brown sugar	
30 mL	2 tbsp	butter, melted	coconut oil, melted
3 mL	½ tsp	cinnamon	
1 mL	¼ tsp	salt	

IMPLEMENTS

Oven • Large and small mixing bowls • Grater/zester
Baking pan, 9"x9" (23x23 cm)

DIRECTIONS

1. Preheat the oven to 400°F (205°C).

2. In a large mixing bowl, sift together the barley flour, 1 cup (240 mL) of the all-purpose flour, and the salt, sugar and baking powder.
Cut in the margarine *(or coconut oil)*.

3. Add half of the orange peel, the egg *(or flax egg)*, ½ cup (120 mL) of the orange juice, and the milk *(or soy milk)*. Stir until blended.

4. Spread the batter into a greased 9"x9" (23x23 cm) baking pan.

5. In a small mixing bowl, combine the remaining all-purpose flour, the brown sugar, the melted butter *(or coconut oil)*, the remaining orange juice, the remaining orange peel, and the cinnamon and salt.

6. Mix until well blended.

7. Sprinkle the topping over the batter.

8. Bake for 25–30 minutes.

Yields 9 servings.

 COCONUT BROWNIES

These brownies can be topped with chocolate frosting if desired, but already taste great on their own!

INGREDIENTS

360 mL	1½ cups	barley flour
2 mL	½ tsp	baking soda
2 mL	½ tsp	salt
60 mL	¼ cup	water
240 mL	1 cup	sugar
120 mL	½ cup	canola margarine
120 mL	½ cup	butter
480 mL	2 cups	semi-sweet chocolate chips
5 mL	1 tsp	vanilla
	4	eggs
240 mL	1 cup	flaked coconut
240 mL	1 cup	chopped walnuts

IMPLEMENTS

Oven • Stove • Large and small mixing bowls • Small saucepan
Baking pan, 15"x10" (38x25 cm)

DID YOU KNOW?

There are reports that barley may have positive effects on the immune system, but these benefits are still being scientifically investigated. (See G.F. Fox in the Bibliography on page 370.)

DIRECTIONS   :55

❶ Preheat the oven to 325°F (165°C).

❷ In a large bowl, sift together the flour, baking soda, and salt.
Set aside.

❸ In a small saucepan, combine the water, sugar, margarine, and butter.
Stir constantly over low heat until the margarine and butter are melted.

❹ Remove the butter mixture from the heat.
Por the butter mixture into the flour mixture to create the batter.
Add the chocolate chips and vanilla to the batter.
Stir until well-blended.

❺ In a small bowl, beat the eggs.
Add the beaten eggs, coconut, and nuts to the batter.
Mix the batter thoroughly.

❻ Spread the batter into a greased 15"×10" (38×25 cm) baking pan.

❼ Bake for 30 minutes.

❽ Allow the brownies to cool, then cut into rectangles.

Yields 24 brownies.

ⓥ 🌾 TOLL HOUSE SQUARES

These treats will be a hit with all ages. We used to take them on camping trips and they were all eaten before we reached the campground.

INGREDIENTS   *VEGAN*

60 mL	¼ cup	**butter**			
		or...	120 mL	½ cup	**coconut oil**
60 mL	¼ cup	**canola margarine**			*(leave out margarine)*
90 mL	6 tbsp	**sugar**			
90 mL	6 tbsp	**brown sugar**			
150 mL	10 tbsp	**barley flour**			
120 mL	½ cup	**all-purpose flour**			
5 mL	1 tsp	**baking soda**			
2 mL	½ tsp	**salt**			
	1	**egg**			flax egg
5 mL	1 tsp	**vanilla**			
120 mL	½ cup	**chopped walnuts**			
240 mL	1 cup	**chocolate chips**			**non-dairy chocolate chips**

IMPLEMENTS

Oven • Large mixing bowl • Sieve • Baking pan, 8"×8" (20×20 cm)

DID YOU KNOW?

Wheat and rye are in the same plant family as barley, and were probably developed as food grains around the same time as barley. Early on, barley became the preferred grain for making fermented drinks, but archeological evidence shows that barley seeds were also ground in crude stone mills, made into patties, and baked as flatbreads. Barley foods are mentioned in several places in the Bible.

DIRECTIONS

:30

1 Preheat the oven to 350°F (175°C).

2 **Non-vegan:** Melt the butter and margarine and combine them in a mixing bowl along with the sugar and brown sugar.

   Vegan: Melt the coconut oil and combine it in a mixing bowl with the sugar and brown sugar.

3 Sift the barley flour, all-purpose flour, baking soda, and salt into the butter *(or coconut oil)* mixture.

4 Add the egg *(or flax egg)* and the vanilla.
   Mix well.

5 Stir in the chopped walnuts until blended together.

6 Pour the batter into a greased 8"×8" (20×20 cm) baking pan.
   Spread the chocolate chips over the top.

7 Bake for 2–3 minutes.

8 Remove the pan from the oven and cut the chocolate chips into the batter to create a marbled effect.

9 Bake for another 10–12 minutes, or until done.

Yields 9 bars.

ⓥ 🌾 FIG BARS

This recipe was developed by my daughter Jean, who loved to bake.

INGREDIENTS   *VEGAN*

240 mL	1 cup	**figs**, chopped (8 oz)	
120 mL	½ cup	**water**	
90 mL	6 tbsp	**canola margarine**	coconut oil
120 mL	½ cup	**brown sugar**	
300 mL	1¼ cups	**barley flour**	
240 mL	1 cup	**all-purpose flour**	
1 mL	¼ tsp	**salt**	
2 mL	½ tsp	**baking soda**	
60 mL	¼ cup	**hot water**	

IMPLEMENTS

Oven • Stove • Blender • Small saucepan • Mixing bowl ×2
Wax paper • Cookie sheet

DID YOU KNOW?

There's indisputable evidence that increasing consumption of barley on a daily basis lowers blood cholesterol, and thus reduces the incidence of heart disease and diabetes.

DIRECTIONS

1. Preheat the oven to 350°F (175°C).

2. In a small saucepan, cook the figs in the water until the water is absorbed.

3. Using a blender, blend the figs into a paste.
   Set the fig paste aside to cool.

4. In a mixing bowl, cream together the margarine *(or coconut oil)* and sugar.

5. In a separate bowl, mix together the barley flour, all-purpose flour, salt, and baking soda.

6. Add the dry mixture and ¼ cup (60 mL) of hot water to the creamed mixture, alternating between small amounts of each while mixing.

7. Form the dough into a ball and chill it.

8. Divide the dough ball into two halves.
   Between two sheets of wax paper (to prevent sticking), roll each half of the dough ball into an 8"x9" (20x23 cm) rectangle.

9. Transfer one rectangle of dough onto a greased cookie sheet.
   Spread the fig paste on top of the dough.
   Place the other rectangle of dough on top of the fig paste.

10. Press the edges of the dough together.
    Score the dough into bars

11. Bake for 30 minutes.

Yields 15 bars.

 LEMON SQUARES

These lemon squares are tangy and delicious, and the combination of whole wheat and barley flour provides extra nutrients and fiber.

INGREDIENTS

240 mL	1 cup	whole wheat flour
240 mL	1 cup	barley flour
120 mL	½ cup	canola margarine
120 mL	½ cup	butter
120 mL	½ cup	powdered sugar
	3	eggs
480 mL	2 cups	sugar
5 mL	1 tsp	baking powder
2 mL	½ tsp	salt
80 mL	⅓ cup	lemon juice
5 mL	1 tsp	lemon peel

IMPLEMENTS

Oven • Small mixing bowl x2 • Baking pan, 9"x13" (23x33 cm)

DID YOU KNOW?

Fat is used by our body as a compact source of energy. Compared to protein or carbohydrates, the average fat contains 2½ times as many calories per weight.

DIRECTIONS

1. Preheat the oven to 350°F (175°C).

2. In a small mixing bowl, combine the whole wheat flour, barley flour, margarine, butter, and powdered sugar.

3. Press the mixture into a 9"x13" (23x33 cm) baking pan.
   Bake for 20 minutes.
   Remove the pan from the oven.

4. Beat together the eggs, sugar, baking powder, salt, lemon juice, and the lemon peel.
   Pour the lemon mixture over top of the crust.

5. Bake for another 20–25 minutes.

6. Remove the pan from the oven and allow it to cool.

7. Cut into squares.

Yields 24 squares.

Ⓥ 🌾 PUMPKIN PIE BARS

This is more than a cookie, it's a whole dessert on its own.

INGREDIENTS

VEGAN

240 mL	1 cup	**barley flour**	
240 mL	1 cup	**barley flakes**	
240 mL	1 cup	**brown sugar**	
150 mL	10 tbsp	**canola margarine**	coconut oil
480 mL	2 cups	**canned pumpkin**	
380 g	13.5 oz	**evaporated milk**	coconut milk
	2	**eggs**	flax eggs
180 mL	¾ cup	**sugar**	
2 mL	½ tsp	**salt**	
5 mL	1 tsp	**cinnamon**	
3 mL	½ tsp	**ginger**	
1 mL	¼ tsp	**cloves**	
360 mL	1½ cups	**nuts**, chopped	

IMPLEMENTS

Oven • Mixing bowls: medium x2, small
Baking pan, 9"x13" (23x23 cm)

DIRECTIONS

1. Preheat the oven to 350°F (175°C).

2. In a small bowl, combine the barley flour, barley flakes, ½ cup (120 mL) of the brown sugar, and ½ cup (120 mL) of the margarine *(or coconut oil)*. Mix untril crumbly.

3. Press the mixture into an ungreased 9"x13" (23x23 cm) baking pan.

4. Bake for 15 minutes.

5. Meanwhile, mix together the pumpkin, evaporated milk *(or coconut milk)*, eggs *(or flax eggs)*, sugar, salt, cinnamon, ginger, and cloves.

6. After 15 minutes, remove the pan from the oven.
   Pour the pumpkin mixture over the baked crust.

7. Bake for another 20 minutes.

8. Remove the pan from the oven.

9. In a mixing bowl, combine the nuts, the remaining brown sugar, and the remaining margarine *(or coconut oil)*.
   Sprinkle the nut mixture over the baked pumpkin.

10. Bake for another 20 minutes, or until the mixture is set.
    Cut into squares.

Yields 24 bars.

v 🌾 CARROT BARS

Nutritious and tasty, a great snack for active youngsters..

INGREDIENTS

			VEGAN
180 mL	¾ cup	**light brown sugar**	
60 mL	¼ cup	**canola margarine**	coconut oil
	1	**egg**	flax egg
480 mL	2 cups	**carrot**, shredded	
5 mL	1 tsp	**vanilla**	
240 mL	1 cup	**whole wheat flour**	
5 mL	1 tsp	**baking powder**	
5 mL	1 tsp	**cinnamon**	
1 mL	¼ tsp	**salt**	
180 mL	¾ cup	**barley flakes**	
120 mL	½ cup	**raisins**	
30 mL	2 tbsp	**wheat germ**	

IMPLEMENTS

Oven • Large mixing bowl • Baking pan, 9"x9" (23x23 cm)

DID YOU KNOW?

Mugicha (barley tea) is a popular drink in Japan, China, and Korea. Consumed either hot or cold, it is made from ground roasted barley, usually pearl barley, similarly to regular tea.

DIRECTIONS :50

1. Preheat the oven to 350°F (175°C).

2. In a large mixing bowl, combine the brown sugar, margarine *(or coconut oil)*, and egg *(or flax egg)*.
   Cream the mixture together until light and fluffy.

3. Add the carrots and vanilla.
   Mix everything until well-blended.

4. Add the whole wheat flour, baking powder, cinnamon, and salt.
   Mix everything together.

5. Stir in the barley flakes, raisins, and wheat germ.

6. Spread the batter into a lightly-greased 9"×9" (23×23 cm) baking pan.

7. Bake for 30 minutes.

8. Remove the pan and allow it to cool.
   Cut into squares.

Yields 9 servings.

Ⓥ 🌾 ZUCCHINI BARS

These bars have vegetable fiber as well as barley flakes and yummy chocolate chips.

INGREDIENTS

			VEGAN
120 mL	½ cup	canola margarine	coconut oil
180 mL	¾ cup	brown sugar	
	2	eggs	flax eggs
240 mL	1 cup	zucchini, grated	
5 mL	1 tsp	vanilla	
240 mL	1 cup	all-purpose flour	
240 mL	1 cup	barley flakes	
2 mL	½ tsp	baking powder	
2 mL	½ tsp	baking soda	
120 mL	½ cup	raisins	
180 mL	¾ cup	semi-sweet choc. chips	non-dairy choc. chips

IMPLEMENTS

Oven • Large and small mixing bowls • Baking pan, 9"x13" (23x33 cm)

DIRECTIONS

1 Preheat the oven to 350°F (175°C).

2 In a large mixing bowl, cream the margarine *(or coconut oil)* together with the brown sugar.

3 Stir in the eggs *(or flax eggs)*, zucchini, and vanilla.

4 In a small bowl, combine the flour, barley flakes, baking powder, baking soda, raisins, and chocolate chips.

5 Add the flour mixture to the creamed mixture.
Stir together until well-blended.

6 Pour the batter into a greased 9"×13" (23×33 cm) baking pan.

7 Bake for 25 minutes.

8 Remove the pan and allow it to cool.
Cut into bars.

Yields 20 bars.

⊙ ♨ CHOCOLATE PEANUT SQUARES

These are a hit with Snickers lovers!

INGREDIENTS

VEGAN

120 mL	½ cup	barley flour	
120 mL	½ cup	light brown sugar	
1 mL	¼ tsp	baking soda	
1 mL	¼ tsp	salt	
240 mL	1 cup	unsalted roasted peanuts, coarsely chopped	
90 mL	6 tbsp	canola margarine	coconut oil
	2 squares	unsweetened chocolate	
	1	egg	flax egg
180 mL	¾ cup	sugar	
160 mL	⅔ cup	all-purpose flour	
2 mL	½ tsp	baking powder	
60 mL	¼ cup	milk	soy milk
10 mL	2 tsp	vanilla	
170 g	6 oz	low fat cream cheese	

or...

180 mL	¾ cup	raw cashews
15 mL	1 tbsp	lemon juice
2 mL	½ tsp	salt
30 mL	2 tbsp	water

60 mL	¼ cup	confectioner's sugar

IMPLEMENTS

Oven • Stove • Blender • Heavy saucepan • Medium saucepan
Mixing bowls: large, medium, and small
Baking pan, 8"x8"x2" (20x20x5 cm)

recipe continues on page 342 ▶

▶ **Chocolate Peanut Squares,** *continued from 340.*

DIRECTIONS *1:20*

① Preheat the oven to 350°F (175°C).

② **Vegan:** Soak the raw cashews in hot water for 1 hour.
Drain the cashews and blend them together with the lemon juice and salt.
If necessary, add more water to achieve a smooth consistency.
Put the mixture in the fridge.

③ In a bowl, combine the barley flour, brown sugar, baking soda and salt.

④ In a small saucepan, melt 4 tbsp (90 mL) of the canola margarine *(or coconut oil)*.

⑤ Meanwhile, in a blender, coarsely chop the peanuts.
Add the peanuts to the flour mixture.

⑥ Add the melted margarine *(or melted coconut oil)* to the mixture and stir until blended.

⑦ Press the mixture into a greased 8"x8"x2" (20x20x5 cm) baking pan.
Set the pan aside.

8. In a heavy saucepan, melt together the remaining margarine *(or coconut oil)* and the 2 squares of unsweetend chocolate.

9. In a large mixing bowl, use a hand mixer to beat together the egg *(or flax egg)* and the sugar for 2 minutes.

10. Remove the chocolate from the heat.
Beat the chocolate mixture into the egg mixture.

11. In a small bowl, combine the all-purpose flour, baking powder, and salt.

12. Stir the flour mixture and the milk *(or soy milk)* into the chocolate mixture, alternating between the two.
Stir in 1 tsp (5 mL) of the vanilla.

13. Spread the chocolate mixture evenly over the nut mixture in the pan.

14. Bake at 350°F (175°C) for 25–30 minutes.

15. Remove the pan from the oven and allow it to cool for 10 minutes.

16. Bring the cream cheese *(or cashew mixture)* to room temperature.
Beat it together with the confectioner's sugar and the remaining vanilla until smooth.

17. While the chocolate layer is still slightly warm, spread the frosting over top.

18. Cut into squares.

Yields 16 squares.

QUICK BARLEY PUDDING

This is a modern-day convenience recipe for an old-time dish—tasty and nutritious.

INGREDIENTS   *VEGAN*

240 mL	1 cup	**pearl barley**
480 mL	2 cups	**water**
240 mL	1 cup	**chopped walnuts**
7 mL	1½ tsp	**cinnamon**
105 g	3¾ oz	**regular cook vanilla pudding mix** (1 package)
	or...	*(use vegan pudding mix)*
540 mL	2¼ cups	**milk** **soy milk**
120 mL	½ cup	**raisins**
30 mL	2 tbsp	**sugar**
4 mL	¾ tsp	**vanilla**

IMPLEMENTS

Stove • Large saucepan

DIRECTIONS   *1:00*

❶ In a large saucepan, combine the barley, water, walnuts, and cinnamon.

❷ Bring the barley to a boil.
Cover, reduce heat, and simmer 40 minutes, or until the barley is tender.

❸ Sprinkle the pudding mix and raisins over the barley.

❹ Increase the heat.
Gradually add the milk (or soy milk).
Stir constantly, until the mixture comes to a boil.

❺ Remove the pudding from the heat and stir in the sugar and vanilla.
Chill before serving.

Yields 10 servings.

 BARLEY RICE CUSTARD

A nutritious and delicious dessert.

INGREDIENTS

160 mL	⅔ cup	**white rice**
160 mL	⅔ cup	**pearl barley**
5 mL	1 tsp	**salt**
630 mL	2⅔ cups	**water**
600 mL	2½ cups	**milk**
1 mL	¼ tsp	**salt**
180 mL	¾ cup	**sugar**
10 mL	2 tsp	**vanilla**
	4	**eggs**
5 mL	1 tsp	**lemon peel**

IMPLEMENTS

Oven • Stove • Casserole dish • Large saucepan • Grater/zester

DIRECTIONS   *1:55*

❶ Preheat the oven to 325°F (165°C).

❷ In a large saucepan, combine the rice, barley, 1 tsp (5 mL) of salt, and the water. Cook until the water is absorbed.

❸ Add the milk, remaining salt, sugar, vanilla, eggs, and lemon peel. Stir until well-blended.

❹ Pour the custard into a casserole dish.

❺ Bake for 1 hour.

❻ Chill the custard before serving.

Yields 6 servings.

TOASTED BARLEY MERINGUE PUDDING

This is reminiscent of a flaky custard. The original recipe contained brandy in place of vanilla.

INGREDIENTS

360 mL	1½ cups	barley flakes
840 mL	3½ cups	milk
	4	eggs
120 mL	½ cup	sugar
10 mL	2 tsp	vanilla
3 mL	½ tsp	cinnamon
1 mL	¼ tsp	salt
75 mL	5 tbsp	sugar

IMPLEMENTS

Oven • Stove • Baking sheet • Large saucepan • Hand mixer
Large and small mixing bowls

DID YOU KNOW?

Barley contains *tocotrienol*, a close relative of vitamin E. If the tocotrienol in barley is extracted and concentrated, it can be used to help normalize blood cholesterol.

DIRECTIONS

1 Preheat the oven to 350°F (175°C).

2 Toast the barley flakes on a baking sheet for 10–15 minutes.

3 In a large saucepan, combine the toasted barley flakes and the milk.
Bring to a boil.
Reduce the heat to low and stir for 10 minutes.
Remove the barley from the heat.

4 Separate the egg yolks from the whites.
In a small mixing bowl, beat the yolks until fluffy.
Set the egg whites aside.

5 Add ½ cup (120 mL) of the sugar to the beaten egg yolks.
Beat together for 5 minutes.

6 Add the yolk mixture to the barley and milk.
Cook over medium heat, stirring constantly, for 7 minutes, or until thickened.

7 Blend in the vanilla, cinnamon, and salt.
Pour the barley into a large mixing bowl and chill it.

8 With a hand mixer, beat the egg whites at high speed.
Add 5 tbsp (75 mL) of sugar, 1 tbsp (15 mL) at a time, beating after each addition until soft peaks are formed.
Spread the meringue mix over the pudding.

9 Bake for 10 minutes, or until golden brown.

Yields 8 servings.

APPLE PUDDING

This is an old, traditional Scandinavian dessert. Tastes great topped with whipped cream!

INGREDIENTS

	4	apples
480 mL	2 cups	water
15 mL	1 tbsp	lemon juice
120 mL	½ cup	quick-cooking barley
1 mL	¼ tsp	salt
120 mL	½ cup	raisins
180 mL	¾ cup	sugar
3 mL	½ tsp	cinnamon
½ mL	⅛ tsp	mace

IMPLEMENTS

Oven • Stove • Casserole dish • Saucepan

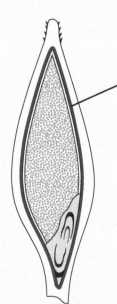

DID YOU KNOW?

Under the hull, the endosperm is surrounded by the *bran*.

The bran gives extra protection to the endosperm. It consists of layers of fiber, along with enzymes used during germination (sprouting). These enzymes are nutritious (high-quality) proteins.

DIRECTIONS

1. Preheat the oven to 375°F (190°C).

2. Pare, peel, and slice the apples.
   Place them in an oven safe casserole dish.

3. Add 1 cup (240 mL) of water and the lemon juice.

4. Cover and bake for 30 minutes.

5. In the meantime, combine the barley, remaining water, and salt in a
   saucepan. Cook for 15 minutes.

6. Remove the barley from the heat.
   Add the raisins, sugar, cinnamon and mace.
   Stir until blended.

7. Pour the barley over the apples.

8. Bake for an additional 30 minutes.

Yields 8 servings.

Ⓥ 🌾 KRENTJE BRIJ

This recipe for Dutch fruit pudding was provided from a local Dutch festival that is held every year in Montana.

INGREDIENTS   *VEGAN*

240 mL	1 cup	pearl barley	
240 mL	1 cup	raisins	
960 mL	4 cups	water	
80 mL	⅓ cup	honey	maple syrup
170 g	6 oz	raspberry gelatin	*(use vegan gelatin)*
960 mL	4 cups	grape juice	

IMPLEMENTS

Stove • Large saucepan • Large mixing bowl

DIRECTIONS   4:25

❶ In a large saucepan, combine the pearl barley, raisins, and water.

❷ Cook over medium heat for 2–2½ hours.

❸ Add the honey *(or maple syrup)*, gelatin, and grape juice.

❹ Bring the mixture to a boil.

❺ Remove the mixture from the heat and pour it into a large bowl. Chill before serving.

Yields about 10 servings.

SUGGESTIONS

Try adding frozen raspberries, currants, or currants with raisins.
For adults only, try a combination of grape juice and wine.

⊙ 🌾 APPLE CRISP

A well-loved classic best served warm. For a festive touch, add whipped cream.

INGREDIENTS   *VEGAN*

6		**apples**, tart	
630 mL	2⅔ cups	**brown sugar**	
120 mL	½ cups	**barley flour**	
120 mL	½ cups	**barley flakes**	
4 mL	¾ tsp	**cinnamon**	
4 mL	¾ tsp	**nutmeg**	
80 mL	⅓ cup	**canola margarine**	**coconut oil**

IMPLEMENTS

Oven • Small mixing bowl • Baking pan, 9"×9" (23×23 cm)

DIRECTIONS   :55

1. Preheat the oven to 350°F (175°C).

2. Peel, pare, and slice the apples to obtain 4 cups (940 mL) of slices. Place the apples in greased 9"×9" (23×23 cm) baking pan.

3. In a small mixing bowl, combine the brown sugar, flour, flakes, cinnamon, nutmeg, and margarine. Blend until the mixture is crumbly.

4. Spread the flour mixture over the apples.

5. Bake for 30–35 minutes, or until the apples are tender and the topping is golden brown.

Yields 8 servings.

ⓥ ⚜ PEACH PECAN CRISP

When peaches are in season, this is a terrific dessert. Try it with whipped cream to make it extra-special!

INGREDIENTS   *VEGAN*

960 mL	4 cups	**peaches**, peeled and sliced	
60 mL	¼ cup	**honey**	maple syrup
15 mL	1 tbsp	**peach brandy** (optional)	
2 mL	½ tsp	**vanilla**	
1 mL	¼ tsp	**cinnamon**	
120 mL	½ cup	**barley flour**	
60 mL	¼ cup	**brown sugar**	
½ mL	⅛ tsp	**salt**	
45 mL	3 tbsp	**canola margarine**	coconut oil
120 mL	½ cup	**pecans**, chopped	

IMPLEMENTS

Oven • Casserole pan, 2 qt (1.89 L) • Small mixing bowl

DIRECTIONS   :55

❶ Preheat the oven to 375°F (190°C).

❷ Coat a 2 qt. (1.89 L) casserole dish with cooking spray.
Blend the peaches, honey *(or maple syrup)*, peach brandy, vanilla, and cinnamon in the dish.

❸ In a small mixing bowl, combine the flour, brown sugar, and salt.
Cut the margarine into the flour mixture until it resembles coarse meal.
Stir the pecans into the flour mixture.

❹ Sprinkle the flour mixture evenly over the peaches.

❺ Bake for 30 minutes, or until lightly browned and bubbly.

Yields 6 servings.

Ⓥ 🌾 SCOTTISH APPLE BUNS

Try serving these buns warm, with powdered sugar sprinkled over the top.

INGREDIENTS   *VEGAN*

240 mL	1 cup	**barley flour**	
240 mL	1 cup	**all-purpose flour**	
5 mL	1 tsp	**cream of tartar**	
2 mL	½ tsp	**baking soda**	
1 mL	¼ tsp	**salt**	
60 mL	¼ cup	**canola margarine**	**coconut oil**
60 mL	¼ cup	**sugar**	
	1	**egg**	
or...	7 mL	½ tbsp	**ground flaxseed**
	45 mL	3 tbsp	**apple sauce**
30 mL	2 tbsp	**water**	
240 mL	1 cup	**apple sauce**, preferably home made	
5 mL	1 tsp	**cinnamon**	

IMPLEMENTS

Oven • Muffin pan • Large and medium mixing bowls

DIRECTIONS

1. Preheat the oven to 425°F (220°C).

2. In a large mixing bowl, sift the barley flour, all-purpose flour, cream of tartar, baking soda, and salt.

3. Cut in the margarine (or coconut oil) and toss the dough until it's the consistency of breadcrumbs.

4. Add the sugar, egg (or flax egg), and water.
   Blend everything together until the dough is stiff, but not sticky.

5. Divide the dough in half.
   Roll the first half of the dough out to ¼" (6 mm) thick.

6. Cut the dough into rounds that will fit into muffin tins.
   Place each round in a greased muffin tin.

7. Mix together the applesauce and cinnamon.
   Put an equal amount of applesauce on each round of dough.

8. Roll out the remaining dough slightly thicker than the first half.
   Cut out smaller rounds and place each one on top of the apple sauce.

9. Bake for 10–15 minutes.

Yields 6 buns.

❧ REFERENCES ❧

BARLEY WATER

Barley Water may be beneficial in preventing mouth sores and intestinal upsets during chemotherapy.

Little research has been done on barley water, and most claims are only anecdotes, rather than clinical evidence. However, we (the authors) have witnessed the effects of barley water and are convinced of its benefits.

Prepare barley water using the guidelines below. (Although whole waxy hulless barley is recommended, any hulless or pearl barley may be used.)

INGREDIENTS

120 mL	½ cup	**whole waxy hulless barley**
2400 mL	2½ qt	**water**
120 mL	½ cup	**sugar**, **honey**, or **other sweetener** (if desired)
		lemon juice (if desired)

DIRECTIONS   *8:00*

1 In a saucepan, combine the water and barley.
Cook at a simmer overnight, or for 8 hours.

🕐   *... after 8 hours ...*

2 Strain the barley kernels from the water.
(The cooked barley can be used in another recipe if desired.)

3 Add sugar and lemon juice for flavour.

Chill and keep refrigerated.

Sip during chemotherapy, and throughout days of therapy. The water may be quite thick, and may also be pinkish in color, depending on the variety of barley used.

⚜ LOWERING BLOOD CHOLESTEROL

The best barley to use for this recipe is whole kernels or flakes of waxy hulless barley. However, any barley can be used if the hull is removed.

Grind the barley in a blender or food processor until it's the consistency of corn meal (a coarse powder). Store the barley meal in the refrigerator until ready to use.

To use the barley meal, mix 2–3 tbsp (30–45 mL) of the barley meal with apple sauce, yogurt, or any other moist food.

Consume the blend just before your meal. This allows the soluble fiber (beta-glucan) to interact with the other foods.

Following this regime, total and LDL cholesterol can usually be lowered.

If you experience diarrhea or other intestinal discomfort, stop eating the barley mixture for a day. Then, gradually reintroduce it with your meals.

 VEGAN PREPARATIONS

Some recipes call for substitutes that are more complicated than a single ingredient or two. These common substitutes are described below.

Flax Eggs

Flax eggs are used as a vegan substitute for eggs in certain recipes. Follow this simple recipe to create one flax egg:

INGREDIENTS

15 mL	1 tbsp	**ground flaxseeds**
45 mL	3 tbsp	**water**

DIRECTIONS   :20

① Mix flaxseeds and water.
Place in refrigerator for 15 minutes

Cashew Cream

Some recipes in this book call for a cashew-based cream as a substitute for cream cheese or sour cream. Although this cream is always made with the same ingredients, the proportions have been customized for each recipe to give the best possible result. Follow the instructions provided, paying careful attention to the amounts of each ingredient, to achieve the right texture and consistency.

Cashew Powder

This is a substitute for parmesan cheese, using a slightly different recipe and forming a powder instead of a cream. Again, proportions vary, so follow the instructions for the particular recipe.

GUIDE TO VEGAN INGREDIENTS

If you haven't made a vegan recipe before, some of the ingredients may be unfamiliar to you. This section explains how some common vegan ingredients are used, what to look for when buying them, and how to store and handle them.

Apple Cider Vinegar

This is a type of vinegar, produced by fermentation of apple cider, that has several uses in vegan cooking. Mixed with soy milk, it can be used to create a substitute for butter, margarine, or buttermilk. Apple cider vinegar is also used in the Cashew Cream recipe mentioned above.

Look for organic apple cider vinegar in a glass bottle, with "mother" or "mother of vinegar" (a sediment remaining from the fermentation process). Store at room temperature in a cool dark place before and after opening. In some areas, apple cider vinegar may be known as "cider vinegar" or "ACV".

Brown Rice Syrup

This is used as a plant-based substitute for honey in vegan cooking. It has a glycemic index of 98, which is higher than table sugar (65) and similar to glucose (100).

Look for brown rice syrup in Asian grocery stores, health food stores, or your local grocery store (in the appropriate aisle). It may also be called rice syrup, rice malt, or maltose syrup depending on your area.

Store at room temperature in a cool dark place before and after opening. It has a shelf life of about one year.

Coconut Butter

A butter substitute, similar in use to coconut oil.

Coconut butter can be found in health food stores. Store at room temperature in a cool, dark place before and after opening.

Coconut Milk

Coconut milk is the liquid produced by grating the meat of a brown coconut. It's often used as a substitute for milk and other dairy products in vegan cooking.

Do not confuse coconut milk with coconut water or coconut juice. Coconut water or juice is a clear, watery liquid often marketed as a beverage, whereas coconut milk is a whitish, thicker liquid (similar in consistency to cow's milk), with a higher fat content.

Look for coconut milk in cans labelled "BPA free". Refrigerate after opening and use within several days.

Coconut Oil

This is typically used as a substitute for butter or margarine in vegan cooking. Despite the name, it is firm (not free-flowing) at room temperature. Some recipes call for melted coconut oil; the oil can be melted on the stove in a saucepan on medium-low heat.

Coconut oil contains high levels of saturated fatty acids, and its effects on cholesterol are still being studied. As a result, some health authorities advise against consuming it regularly. Its use in the vegan recipes in this book is generally limited to small amounts as a non-animal substitute for butter or margarine.

Look for unrefined, extra-virgin coconut oil in a glass jar. Store at room temperature in a cool, dark place before and after opening. In warmer months, the oil may melt in its container—this is not a concern.

Maple Syrup

Like brown rice syrup, this is used as a plant-based substitute for honey in vegan cooking. Store in the fridge once opened.

Non-Dairy Yogurt (Soy Yogurt, Cultured Coconut)

There are many non-dairy yogurts available. If the recipe calls specifically for soy yogurt, use that. Otherwise, any non-dairy yogurt is acceptable, though we recommend cultured coconut yogurt (and have noted this in the ingredients). Handle non-dairy yogurt the same way you would normal yogurt.

Nutritional Yeast

A deactivated yeast with a strong flavour described as nutty, cheesy, or creamy. Nutritional yeast is often used in place of cheese in vegan cooking, and is an ingredient in the Cashew Powder mentioned above.

Nutritional yeast can be found in bulk food stores and sometimes in packages. It will typically come in the form of flakes or a yellow powder. Do not confuse nutritional yeast with yeast extract, which is a dark brown paste with a very strong flavour.

Nutritional yeast can be stored alongside spices.

Seitan

Made from gluten (the main protein of wheat), seitan is often used in vegan cooking as a meat substitute. The texture of seitan is often more chewy or stringy than tofu. Seitan can sometimes be difficult to find—try a specialty health food store if necessary.

Refrigerate unused portions covered in vegetable broth in a glass container. Can be kept one week.

Soy Milk, Soy Cream

Soy milk is manufactured by soaking dry soybeans and grinding them in water. It has about the same amount of protein as cow's milk, and is often used in vegan cooking as a substitute for milk. It is also a staple of East Asian cuisine. Soy milk does not contain lactose, so it is appropriate for people who are lactose-intolerant.

When shopping for soy milk, look for organic, unsweetened milk. There should be no ingredients other than soybeans and water. Do not substitute almond milk or other non-soy plant milks. Most almond milks contain additives (such as carrageenan) that may throw off recipes.

In some areas, soy milk may be called "soy beverage" or "soy drink", either because of tradition, or because of local laws that restrict the term "milk" to specifically animal milk or cow milk. Soy milk powder (used in some recipes in this book) may also be labelled as "dry soy milk".

Tempeh

Tempeh is also made from soybeans, but uses the entire bean, giving it more protein, dietary fiber, and vitamin content. Tempeh is firm and has a different texture than tofu; its typical use in vegan cooking is as a meat analogue.

Tightly wrap unused portions and store in the fridge for 2 days.

Tofu

Tofu is made by coagulating soy milk and pressing the curds into a solid block. Tofu has a subtle flavour and can be used in both savory and sweet dishes, and can also be marinated.

Tofu is a staple of Asian cuisine, where it is used alongside meat and prepared in many ways. In Western countries, tofu is often associated with vegan/vegetarian cuisine. Because of its high protein content, it is often used by vegans and vegetarians as a regular source of protein.

Tofu is produced in several degrees of firmness, including soft or "silken", "firm silken", firm, and extra-firm. The firmest tofu will hold its shape when cooked, while the silken tofu is much softer and is generally only used in sauces and desserts. Be careful to use the correct firmness as called for in the recipe.

Tofu is usually available in your local grocery store, though a larger selection may be available in Asian grocery stores or health food stores.

After opening, refrigerate unused portions, submerged in water, in a glass container. Keep up to two days, changing water daily.

TVP (Texturized Vegetable Protein)

A by-product of extracting soybean oil, TVP is a low-fat, very-high-protein ingredient often used as a meat analogue in vegan cooking. TVP is produced in a variety of textures and is inexpensive.

TVP can be found in larger grocery stores and in health food stores. It may also be labelled as textured soy protein (TSP), soy meat, or soya chunks.

Store TVP in the pantry. Can be stored for up to a year, but will spoil within days if moistened.

Vegan Mayonnaise & Worcestershire Sauce

Vegan substitutes for these ingredients are available, for example, *Veganaise*, *Wizard's Vegan Worcestershire Sauce*, and so on.

 BLOOD CHOLESTEROL

Total Cholesterol

under 200	desirable
200–239	borderline high
over 240	high

Low density / LDL ("bad") cholesterol

under 100	ideal
100–129	optimal, or above optimal
130–159	borderline high
160–189	high
over 190	very high

High density / HDL ("good") cholesterol

under 40	risk factor
over 60	desirable

Values represent milligrams per deciliter (mg/dl). Reference: National Heart, Lung and Blood Institute, National Institutes of Health (www.nhlb.nih.gov).

GLYCEMIC INDEX

The Glycemic Index (GI) is a system of comparing individual foods, based on their direct effect on blood sugar levels. The values for each food are determined by a standardized test, in which subjects consume each test food and their blood sugar levels are measured over a specified period of time.

Pure glucose is set at a value of 100, the highest level. All other food and beverage test results range from 0 to 99. The GI of a food is influenced by the composition of the food (carbohydrate, fiber, protein, and fat), by certain processing methods, or complexity of ingredients.

Foods are also sometimes referred to as having "fast carbs", which would mean a high GI level, or "slow carbs", which refers to a low GI level.

Here are the GI levels of some selected foods:

Food	GI
Corn flakes	84
Bread, white	70
Rice, long grain	56
Banana	55
Bread, whole grain	53
Oatmeal	49
Apple	38
Barley, pearl	25

References:

Brand-Miller, J., et al. The Glucose Revolution Life Plan. Marlowe & Co. 2000, 2001.

Wolever, T.N., et al. Food glycemic index, as given in glycemic index tables, is a significant determinant of glycemic responses elicited by composite breakfast meals. Am. J. Clin. Nutr. 83:1306-1312. 2006.

VITAMIN CONTENT

This table compares nutritionally important vitamins in barley, wheat, and oats. Although the values can vary considerably due to natural deviation, these are accepted average values, given in micrograms per gram (µg/g).

Vitamin	Barley µg/g	Oats µg/g	Wheat µg/g
Vitamin A	-	-	-
Vitamin D	-	-	-
Vitamin K	-	-	-
Vitamin E	48.00	30.00	25.00
Thiamin (B1)	4.40	7.20	4.60
Riboflavin (B2)	1.50	1.70	1.30
Niacin (B3)	72.00	15.10	55.00
Pantothenic acid (B5)	5.70	7.80	9.10
Pyridoxin (B6)	4.40	2.90	4.60
Biotin (B7)	0.13	-	0.06
Folic acid / Folate (B9)	0.40	-	0.60

The data above was taken from Barley Chemistry and Technology, 2nd ed., 2014, AACC International, edited by P.R. Shewry and S.E. Ullrich; Oats Chemistry and Technology 1986, AACC International, edited by F.H. Webster; Wheat Chemistry and Technology 4th ed. 2009, AACC International, edited by K. Khan and P.R. Shewry. Additional reference was made to The Chemistry and Technology of Cereals as Food and Feed, 2nd ed. 1991, an AVI book, Van Nostrand Reinhold, NY., S.A. Matz author.

A dash (-) indicates either that the amount detected was insignificant, or that the substance was not measured/reported in the source, typically because prior studies had shown no significant amount.

MINERAL CONTENT

This table compares nutritionally important minerals in barley, wheat, and oats.

Phytate (phytic acid) phosphorus is noted for two reasons. First, because it causes the other minerals listed to become nutritionally unavailable. The other minerals are irreversibly chemically bound to phytate when the grain is processed (ground). Second, because phytate is not itself nutritionally available; only the non-phytate phosphorus is available.

An exact figure for the phytate phosphorus in barley is not available, but its concentration is similar to that reported in oats (about 75% of the total phosphorus in either grain).

In barley, phytate is concentrated in the outer portion of the kernel. When covered barley is pearled, a large portion of the phytate is removed. This is not the case with hull-less barley (the hull of which is removed during harvesting), unless it is subsequently pearled after harvesting.

The anti-nutritive effect of phytate can be easily overcome by adding a primary source of the affected minerals.

	Barley	Oats	Wheat
Mineral	**ppm**	**ppm**	**ppm**
Total Phosphorus	3000	4300	4200
Phytate Phosphorus	~2250	3200	-
Calcium	250	1170	335
Magnesium	1290	1810	1500
Potassium	4390	5710	3700
Zinc	23	38	40
Iron	28	70	55
Manganese	11	43	56
Copper	4	11	4

The figures above were cited in the text The Chemistry and Technology of Cereals as Food and Feed, 2nd ed. 1991. S. A. Matz, author. Van Nostrand Reinhold. NY.

 BIBLIOGRAPHY

Behall, K.M. and Hallfrisch, J. Effects of barley consumption on CVD risk factors. Cereal Foods World 51:12-15. 2006.

Björck, I., et al. Food properties affecting the digestion and absorption of carbohydrates. Am. J. Clin. Nutr. 59(suppl): 6995-7055. 1994.

Brand-Miller, J. et al., The Glucose Revolution Life Plan. Marlowe & Co. 2000. 2001.

Davidson, A. The Oxford Companion to Food. Oxford University Press. 1999.

FDA. Food and Drug Administration, Federal Register. vol. 71, no. 98, May 22, 2006. Food Labeling: Health Claims: Soluble fiber from certain foods and coronary heart disease. 2006.

Fox, G. J. Immunofiber: Flush Away Disease, Fat and Cholesterol. *www.barleyfood.com*.

Ikegami, S., et al. Effect of boiled barley-rice-feeding on hypercholesterolemic and normo cholesterollemic subjects. Plant Foods Hum. Nutr. 49:317-328. 1996.

Inglis, P. and Whitworth, L. Go Barley: Modern Recipes for an Ancient Grain. Touchwood Editions. Calgary, Canada. 2014.

McIntosh, G., et al. Barley foods and their influence on cholesterol metabolism in: World Review of Nutrition and Dietetics. Karger, Basel, Switzerland. 1995.

Munck, L., et al. Gene for improved nutritional values in barley seed protein. Science 168:198. 1970.

Newman, R. K. and Newman, C. W. Barley for Food and Health, Science, Technology and Products. John Wiley and Sons, Inc. 2008.

Newman, R.K. and Newman, C. W. Barley as a food grain. CFW 36(99):800-805. 1991.

Pomeranz, Y. Food uses of barley. CRC Critical Reviews in Food Technology. 4:377-394. 1974.

Topping, D. L. and Clifton, P. M. Short chain fatty acids and human colonic function: roles of resistant starch and non-starch polysaccharides. Physiol. Rev. 81:1031-1064. 2001.

Ullrich, S.E. ed. Barley: Production, Improvement, and Uses. Blackwell Publishing. 2001.

Wolever, T.N., et al. Food glycemic index, as given in glycemic index tables, is a significant determinant of glycemic responses elicited by composite breakfast meals. Am. J. Clin. Nutr. 83:1306-1312. 2006.

USEFUL WEBSITES

Alberta Barley Commission
www.albertabarley.com

American Diabetes Association
www.diabetes.org

American Heart Association
www.heart.org

American Malting Barley Association
www.AMBAinc.org

Barony Mills
www.birksay.org.uk

CSIRO (Commonwealth Scientific and Industrial Research Organization)
www.csiro.au

Health Canada
www.hc-sc.gc.ca

Idaho Barley Commission
www.barleyidaho.gov

Minnesota Barley Research and Promotion Council
www.mda.state.mn.us/food

Montana Wheat and Barley Committee
www.wbc.agr.mt.gov

National Barley Foods Council
www.barleyfoods.org

National Heart, Lung, and Blood Institute
www.nhlbi.nih.gov

Newman, Walt and Rosemary Blog
www.barleyisbetter.com

Oregon State University Barley Project
www.barleyworld.org

Phoenix Seed Inc.
www.barleyfood.com and www.phoenixseedinc.com

U.S. Food and Drug Administration
www.fda.gov

Wikipedia, the Free Encyclopedia
en.wikipedia.org/wiki/Barley

SUPPLIERS OF BARLEY PRODUCTS

Alaska Flour Company
8107 Wrigley's Fields Road
Delta Junction, AK 99737
907-895-4033
info@alaskaflourcompany.com
(Hulless barley and hulless barley flour)

Arrowhead Mills/Hain-Celestial
110 South Lanton
Hereford, TX 79045
806-364-0730
www.arrowheadmills.com
(Sells barley flour and pearl barley to distributors and online)

Barry Farm Foods
20086 Mudsock Road
Wapakoneta, OH 45895
419-228-4640
order@barryfarm.com
(Wholesale/retail organic barley flour, malt, malt syrup, barley flakes)

Bob's Red Mill Natural Foods, Inc.
13521 SE Pheasant Ct.
Milwaukie, OR 97222
800-349-2173
www.BobsRedMill.com
(Wholesale and retail whole hulless barley, pearled barley, barley flours, grits, and barley flakes)

King Arthur Flour
The Baker's Store
135 Route 5 South
Norwich, VT 05055
800-827-6836
www.KingArthurFlour.com
(Sustagrain barley flakes; Sustagrain is a waxy hulless variety)